Women as Pastors

Creative Leadership Series

Women
as Pastors

Edited by Lyle E. Schaller

Creative Leadership Series
Lyle E. Schaller, Editor

Abingdon / Nashville

To
Miss Ellen Maria Studley

WOMEN AS PASTORS

Copyright © 1982 by Abingdon

Library of Congress Cataloging in Publication Data

Main entry under title:
Women as pastors.
    (Creative leadership series)
    1. Women clergy—United States. I. Schaller, Lyle E. II. Series.
    BV676.W547   253'.2   81-20667   AACR2

ISBN 0-687-45957-5

MANUFACTURED BY THE PARTHENON PRESS AT
NASHVILLE, TENNESSEE, UNITED STATES OF AMERICA

Foreword

Every day the leaders in the churches are faced with complex questions, many of which do not have simple answers.

The Creative Leadership Series was designed to provide these leaders, both lay and clergy, with practical help in responding to some of these questions and in developing a more effective ministry.

One of the questions about which there is still considerable ambivalence and uncertainty is the possibility that "the next minister will be a woman." This possibility is much greater during the 1980s than it was in the 1970s. During the 1970s, the first decade in which women were graduating from theological seminaries and seeking ordination in significant numbers, most of the ordained women in the ministry could be found in one of four areas of service. A disproportionately large number were associate ministers in multiple-staff situations. A substantial number had gone into nonparochial ministries, such as campus ministries, chaplaincies, and other specialized ministries. Approximately fifteen percent shared a pastorate with an ordained husband. The fourth group was composed of women serving small congregations or two- or three-church parishes. Most of these discovered they were the real pioneers, because only a few of these congregations had ever had a female pastor before.

That situation has changed! Today, hundreds of women ministers have a decade or two of experience behind them, and women are serving as district superintendents, senior pastors in large congregations, denominational executives, and seminary professors. The number of women holding the rank of full professor in theological seminaries doubled between the fall of 1976 and September 1981. One woman is a bishop in The United Methodist Church. These changes also have meant that hundreds of middle-sized and larger congregations are now being served by a woman minister, in some cases the second, third, or fourth woman pastor in that congregation's history.

During the 1970s, for the first time, hundreds of Protestant churches on this continent received a new minister who was female. During the 1980s that number will be counted in the thousands and will include many large churches as well as middle-sized ones and smaller congregations.

A reasonable projection is that an association of women who are senior pastors in multiple-staff churches will emerge during the 1980s, flourish, and subsequently begin to decline as these women discover they have more in common in terms of their situation than they do in terms of gender.

As an ordained minister in The United Methodist Church, I expect to live to see the day when a majority of congregations in that denomination will be served by women pastors. That is NOT a prediction that women will outnumber men in the ordained ministry within the foreseeable future.

The basic reason for that projection is the mounting body of evidence that suggests that the pastoral ministry, like many other fields of endeavor, is one in which the natural talents, gifts, and characteristics of women will enable them to excel over their male counterparts. Other such fields might be long-distance swimming, dentistry, needlework, neurosurgery, verbal communication, the assembly of tiny parts, typing, and the accurate perception of the needs of other people.

In brief, the evidence suggests that an increasing number of congregations will be welcoming their first woman pastor during the 1980s, while others will be greeting their second or third female pastor.

This volume is a collection of essays designed to answer some of the questions people have about that possibility. There are many parallels between this book and other volumes in this series. In chapter 11 of his book, *The Small Town Church*, Peter Surrey details the consternation of the female parishioner who discovered that the new acolyte was a girl! In earlier volumes, Robert Kemper offers some sage advice on beginning a new pastorate, and Douglas Johnson deals with the care and feeding of volunteers, both male and female. Speed Leas offers counsel on a subject rarely covered in seminary, the effective management of one's time, while Douglas Walrath provides useful insights on leading churches through change. Many women's first pastorate will be a small church. William Willimon and Robert Wilson have contributed a book to this series on the centrality of preaching and worship in these smaller congregations. In a remarkably sensitive and sensible volume, Donna Sinclair describes the stages in the pilgrimage of a woman married to a pastor. Several women in the ministry also see their pilgrimage as a series of developmental stages.

These and the other books in this series have been designed to answer some of the questions raised by creative leaders when faced with new ideas, unprecedented changes, and a change in tradition. This volume has been planned to encourage congregations to include women in their search when they seek a new pastor. The stories of these pastors should both answer some of the questions that will arise and reassure the skeptics and the doubters that both men and women are called by God to the pastoral ministry.

This book is dedicated to a remarkable minister who has served as an excellent role model to a couple of generations of missionaries and pastors, both male and female.

Lyle E. Schaller
Yokefellow Institute
Richmond, Indiana

Contents

Introduction

"Should we seek a woman as our next pastor?"

"What would happen if we did and she got pregnant? What would we do if that happened?"

"Does God really call women to the ministry?"

"Can a church grow if it has a woman pastor? Our congregation is shrinking and we need to reverse that trend. Doesn't that mean we need a man?"

"What would we call her?"

"What would the people in this community think if our church had a woman pastor?"

"Do you think our church is ready for a woman pastor?"

"Can a woman do the job?"

"What if she is not married?"

"What if she is married? What would we do with her husband?"

These are a few of the questions that come up repeatedly when a congregation is contemplating the possibility of calling a woman as the next pastor.

The chances that a Protestant church on the North American continent will have a woman serving as its next minister have increased very rapidly during the past dozen years. One indicator of the pace of that change is the increase in the number of women enrolled in theological seminaries. According to data collected by the Association of Theological Schools in the United States and Canada, there were 3,358 women enrolled in seminary in 1972. Eight years later this number had more than tripled to 10,830, and women accounted for twenty-two percent of the total enrollment, double the proportion in 1972. Scores of seminaries report that between one-fourth and two-fifths of the candidates for the Master of Divinity degree or the Doctor of Ministry degree are women. It is interesting to note that more than half of the women enrolled for either of those two professional degrees have chosen the in-sequence Doctor of Ministry program in preference to the more traditional Master of Divinity. These facts will provide an answer to some of those who wonder, "If we chose a woman for our next minister, what would we call her?"

The pace of change can be illustrated by looking at a few examples. In 1977, for the first time in that denomination's history, women could be "regularly" ordained in the Episcopal Church. That year 90 women and 96 men were "regularly" ordained as priests in the Episcopal Church.

The Lutheran Church in America began to ordain women in 1970—and during the next seven years, 57 women were ordained. During the following three years, that number increased to 163, and four out of five are serving as parish pastors.

There are more than a thousand ordained women ministers in The United Methodist Church and over five hundred in the several Presbyterian denominations.

Approximately one-half of the clergy in the Salvation Army are women, and several denominations, such as the Church of the Nazarene, the Wesleyan Church, and the

General Council of the Assemblies of God, have a long history of the ordination of women as ministers.

From a historical perspective on American Protestantism, two generalizations stand out that merit consideration when this subject is discussed. First, the greater the sensitivity of a denomination to the oppressed and the downtrodden, and the larger the proportion of the membership that is drawn from among those at the bottom of the social class scale, the greater the probability that that denomination has a long history of accepting women as ministers. With only a few exceptions this basic pattern prevails among both white and black denominations in the United States.

Second, the earliest and the greatest acceptance of women as ordained or commissioned workers in the churches has been on the foreign mission field. In 1910, for example, one third of all missionary physicians were women. As recently as 1929, two thirds of all foreign missionaries under the care of the six largest Protestant denominations in the United States were women. These figures suggest that the possibility that God does call women to full-time Christian service is far from a new concept.

Two of the larger American Pentecostal denominations, the Apostolic Faith and the International Church of the Foursquare Gospel, were founded by women. The revelations of Mrs. Ellen G. White have been central to the Seventh-day Adventists, one of the fastest-growing religious bodies in the world. The Congregational Church authorized the ordination of women in 1853. Several denominations have been ordaining women as ministers for approximately a hundred years, including the American Baptist Churches, the Salvation Army (1880), the Church of God of Anderson, Indiana (1881), the Christian Church

13

(Disciples of Christ, 1888), the Cumberland Presbyterian Church (1890), and the United Brethren in Christ (1889).

There is a long and complex background behind the current increase in the number of women serving in the pastoral ministry, but that will not be discussed here. The central purpose of this book is to provide a resource for the laity who are contemplating the possibility that their next pastor may be a woman. This volume is an attempt to offer real-life responses to the questions that naturally will be raised when that possibility surfaces.

What is the beginning point? There are many. Mary Sue Gast describes how a couple from a church in Michigan came to Iowa to visit, and that was the beginning of that call. Dorothy Fowler was asked by the District Superintendent to serve a church in west Texas. Anne Rosser describes the long period of time she and her husband lived through while seeking a call. Ansley Coe Throckmorton spells out in some detail the anatomy of a call.

Won't there be opposition? Won't some people object to having a woman as their pastor? The answer is, "Yes, certainly!" The content and the nature of some of that opposition is described by Mary Miller-Vikander, who is a pioneer in a denomination that only recently authorized the ordination of women. Anne Rosser shares a similar experience as one of the first women to be ordained in the Southern Baptist Conference. The opposition can be real, but it need not be the controlling factor. These women explain how God's love can melt that opposition.

What if she has a baby? That is one of the most frequently raised objections to women's being in the pastorate. Maribeth Blackman-Sexton tells how one of the older members, after hearing the news that their recently arrived preacher was pregnant, asked, "What do you suppose

14

she'll do now?" Another long-time member replied, "I suppose she'll have a baby in a few months." Janet Gifford-Thorne explains how a minister's pregnancy can be a real asset to a congregation. Mary Sue Gast shares her experiences and points out that she was able to lead the devotional period for the Martha Circle the day before her baby was born—although it might have been more difficult if the Circle had met in the early morning.

"But will a church grow in size and vitality with a woman as the pastor?" That also is a frequently heard question from those who fear that the only churches with women in the pulpit are small congregations. In two radically different situations, Barbara Jurgensen and Janet Gifford-Thorne point out that a woman can help expand the evangelistic outreach of a struggling congregation.

"Well, I guess I can see women serving some churches, but there must be limits on how far they can go." That male chauvinist comment has been heard from both men and women who have reservations about women's being in the ministry. The irrelevance of the observation can be illustrated by Ellen Brubaker's account of the pilgrimage of Marjorie Swank Matthews, the first woman to be elected to the episcopacy in The United Methodist Church. The career of Ansley Coe Throckmorton suggests the ceiling is an imaginary one created by human beings, not by God.

"But do you really think people ever will come to accept a woman as their pastor?" That may be the most widespread reservation about women in the ministry. It is a reservation held by many women as well as by men, by clergy as well as by the laity. In different ways, each of the contributors to this volume has responded to that issue. Dorothy Fowler shares her experience as a bivocational minister who has had to deal with this question in both the high school and the parish. Jane Krauss Jackson, Ansley Coe Throckmorton,

15

and others note that the congregation that is open to having a woman as its next pastor also has some other characteristics that may facilitate acceptance—and that being a woman has some unique advantages.

Perhaps the most perplexing issue for a few is, "What about her husband? If she's married, what kind of expectations do we have of the husband, and what will he expect of us?" One congregation talked about the need to schedule a reception or some similar type of welcoming, "We're glad you're here with us!" event for the new minister's husband, but they couldn't decide whether that was "women's work" or "men's work," so it never happened.

There is no standard response to these questions about the role of the minister's husband, and the variety of men who fill that role may be almost as great as the differences among women married to pastors. Mary Miller-Vikander, Mary Sue Gast, Maribeth Blackman-Sexton, and Anne Rosser speak very directly to this subject for the benefit of those who want to pursue it.

A point that seldom is raised, but is extremely significant, is that many of the women in the pastorate are pursuing a second (or third) career. Many of them bring a wide array of experiences with them when they move into their first pastorate. Dorothy Fowler and Carolyn Jones explain how their experiences in other professions have been a very useful asset for the pastoral ministry. Three-quarters of the writers represented in this volume are in their second or subsequent careers. This list includes Fowler, Throckmorton, Rosser, Matthews, Jones, Jurgensen, and Jackson. They also represent a growing movement in society in general as well as among the people, both male and female, who are entering theological seminaries.

As was pointed out earlier, approximately fifteen percent

of the women in the pastorate are in a co-pastorate with their husbands. Two of these experiences are represented by Anne Rosser and Mary Sue Gast.

Five of the eleven contributors to this volume also have served or are serving as associate ministers in a multiple-staff arrangement. Jones and Miller-Vikander are now serving in that role.

In one way and another all of the eleven contributors to this volume have been pioneers. Each has been "the first" in her present situation. Carolyn Jones identifies some of the feelings and other experiences that are a part of being first.

One of the questions that does come up frequently (but some people are hesitant to raise it openly), is the issue of divorce. The latest projections from the United States Bureau of the Census suggest that forty percent of the married women born during the decade of the 1940s will be divorced at least once during their lifetime. Women going into the ministry are not an exception to that phenomenon. While precise figures are not available, estimates suggest that one third of the married women in the pastoral ministry have been divorced. One third of the women contributing chapters to this volume have been divorced. Is this a handicap?

Several males with responsibilities for ministerial place-ment have observed that a disproportionately large number of the most effective women in the pastorate (a) are mothers, and (b) have been divorced or widowed. Certainly neither is a requirement for a woman to be an effective pastor, but apparently neither is the handicap that some assumed it would be.

How do the laity respond to a woman? Here are two of the responses from the laity in the churches served by the women represented in this volume.

"Your spiritual guidance and style as pastor has been one

17

that has helped us to mature in our faith and ministry. You have been gentle when gentleness was required, firm when firmness needed, and always consistent in your relentless quest to move us toward the fulfillment of our potential."

"When Jane came to us five years ago, our church was 'dying.' I don't believe any of our members really believed we could keep the doors open another year. She brought new life into a small congregation of elderly people."

These are representative of the scores of comments that have been received from lay people as they reflect on their experiences with their first woman pastor.

There are many threads that run through the chapters in this work. These include the experience of being the first woman pastor, the reflections on the structural sexism in the institutional expression of Christianity, and the sense of being on a pilgrimage.

The most impressive common thread, however, is the repeated references to the women's conviction of a call to the ordained ministry. These women express very clearly their Christian convictions, their sense of a call, and their commitment to ministry. Those are the criteria that should dominate any discussion about who our next pastor should be. This book offers brief glimpses into the life and vocational response of eleven women who have heard God's call and have responded. That is the central thread that ties all these chapters together. That call also should be the basic criterion whenever the discussion turns to the qualifications of our "new minister." Yes, women are called by God to the pastoral ministry!

Finally, one cannot help but ask what kinds of responses a book such as this will evoke. The first response we hope to arouse is an increased openness among the laity and the clergy to the idea that women both are called by God to the parish ministry, *and*, as a group, are at least as effective as men in that vocation. Second, we hope to affirm and reinforce the call of women in seminary to the pastoral ministry. Third, we believe this volume can be both informative and freeing to those laywomen, including many mature women contemplating a second career, that a genuine call to the ministry is not only a possibility, but also could be a very fulfilling and satisfying vocation. Fourth, we expect that many women now in the pastorate will find this to be a means of sharing in the experiences of their sisters. Finally, we know we will provoke letters and telephone calls from those who are convinced women should remain in the place they believe God made for them as second-class citizens in a world that was intended to be dominated by men. These letters and telephone calls simply prove that every change worth making carries a price tag.

I

The Dual-Role Pastor

Dorothy Fowler

The summer afternoon, hot and clear, was filled with the fragrance of funeral flowers. I locked the front doors of my church, checked for lights left on in the classrooms, went to my study, and found my robe and ritual book. As I stepped outside into the bright solitude, I was overwhelmed with what a lonely business the ministry is.

"Perhaps," I thought, "if the church were larger, or if the people were younger, if we had more children, if I lived here in town, or if I were male, funerals wouldn't leave me feeling like this." As I started my car, a puff of wind stirred the caliche dust on the parking lot. The sprinkler system on the football practice field across the street began its rhythmic dance, a dog barked somewhere in the distance, and a mourning dove began to call. It was fifty-three miles to home, and I was alone.

I was thirty-nine years old, a full-time teacher in a large high school, the divorced mother of a seventeen-year-old daughter, and the pastor of the United Methodist Church in Wink, a west Texas town whose population (if one could believe the sign at the city limit), was 1053.

Fifty years earlier the sign would have read 20,000 or

more, but those were the days when people were flooding in, drawn by the scent of oil and the clank of machinery to produce it. Perhaps if Wink had become the county seat, or a commercial or transportation center, or had attracted industry, the people would have stayed. But commerce and transportation centered in Odessa, fifty-three miles east, and industry followed. Kermit, eight miles north of Wink, got the courthouse.

As I reached the stop sign in front of the Masonic Lodge Hall, the streets were empty except for a child wobbling along on a bicycle. "Hi, Preacher," he yelled, and then turned back toward the church. As he disappeared, my moment of loneliness disappeared, too. "Preacher." The only word that approaches it for meaning is "teacher." I was the luckiest woman in the world, for both words applied to me, and had since that spring evening in 1976 when the Pastor-Parish Relations Committee at First (and only) United Methodist Church at Wink had met with me.

We had looked each other over very cautiously, they because they had never had a female pastor, and I because I had never been a pastor. Dr. Robert Templeton, then the District Superintendent, had arranged the meeting. He had asked Bob Harrison, pastor of my home church in Odessa, to go to Wink with me as a sort of intermediary. Bob Harrison knew Wink and its Methodists from his days as pastor at Kermit.

"I don't quite remember where the chairperson of Pastor-Parish Relations lives, but if we get there before dark, I can find it," he told me.

It was good that he knew where we were going, for the street markers in Wink had been taken down to be repainted and were not yet back in place. The location system for a stranger in Wink had to be either by direction of the indigenous population or by instinct. I was also glad that he had accompanied me because, instead of meeting with the five members of the Committee, I saw that most of the active church members were present, waiting uneasily to see what the District Superintendent had found at the bottom of the ministerial rag bag.

They seemed less concerned about my gender than about my ministerial competence.

"Can you work with youth?" someone asked.

"I do every day," I replied.

"What will you do about funerals?"

For the first time it occurred to me that someone might actually die, and I would have to conduct the funeral.

"I'll come, of course," I answered.

As the questions continued, I became aware of a deepening pool of sweat forming somewhere around the elastic on my petticoat. By the time the interview ended with their invitation to go see the church building, whose pulpit I would fill for the first time the next Sunday, I was barely able to peel myself off the chair.

As we approached the church, I could see its white stucco walls gleaming in the moonlight. Light flowed from the stained glass windows into the darkness of the back courtyard. As soon as we had seen it all, we prayed together in the foyer, one badly frightened pastor and her courageous congregation, for grace to live with the arrangement we had made.

Pastorates are not made in meetings with the Pastor-Parish Relations Committee nor in prayer circles in the church foyer. They are created in the sharing of life in a community of faith as the fundamental issues of life are faced. People die, get married, are born, have trouble with their children and spats with their neighbors, and pastors share it all. Too often we pastors have no counseling skills

23

beyond a ready and sympathetic ear; nevertheless, people come to us to be comforted and reassured. But if all that people share is crisis, they soon wear each other out. Every congregation needs at least one moment of shared joy.

For us, it became the annual Christmas Eve service, when the church was packed with Christians of every persuasion who wanted to share in the miracle of the Christ Child. Because there is power in ritual, our Christmas Eve service was always the same. The church, dark except for the flickering altar candles and those on the Advent wreath, was filled first with music and then with the words of both prophecy and gospel. When we lighted the Christ candle, for a moment we were united, as denominational and theological differences dimmed in the brilliance of the individual candles that we relighted from the Christ candle. But for the most part, the life of the church, like life at home or at work, is a matter of being faithful to the tasks that must be done.

As my congregation and I built our relationship, I struggled daily with the problem of how to maintain my credibility as a teacher in my classroom. I did not want my students to identify me as a United Methodist preacher, but as a teacher of government, a stern advocate of the separation of church and state. My students, however, frequently heard me preach at my home church in Odessa, and the word spread to students who had no church affiliation. They were understandably curious.

"I hear you are some kind of preacher. Is that right?" one young man asked.

"That's right. Some kind," I answered.

"You like it?"

"Yes."

"Are you any good?"

"I hope so," I told him. "You are welcome to go to Wink sometime and judge for yourself."

Some students did go to Wink, but many more waited until I was preaching at Highland Church in Odessa. In the hall at school one Monday, I met a girl who had heard me preach at Highland the night before. As we passed each other, I overheard her say to the young man who was with her, "That's my preacher."

I turned around to find him staring incredulously. "Are you sure?" he asked. "She looks like a lady to me."

Occasionally students tried to engage me in theological or biblical debate, but those attempts became more and more infrequent as time passed. Most students, most of the time, accepted my dual role in the same way they accepted the color of my hair and my West Texas accent. If they suffered from any of the three, they suffered with quiet grace.

If there were moments of uncertainty about my ministry, they came as a result of neither my parishioners' nor my students' attitudes. They came, instead, as a result of experiences at the Courses of Study School, the Methodist Church's alternative to full-time seminary study. Each summer I spent at Perkins School of Theology on the SMU campus, my brother pastors regaled each other and me with tales of their success. It seemed strange to me that, while the Methodist Church as a whole was losing members, their fabulous churches were doubling or tripling their memberships. Their budgets were skyrocketing. They all seemed to be building new education wings, or buying pipe organs, or, more important, building new parsonages. The new front doors we had put on my church at Wink paled into insignificance as did the new paint and the new carpet. We had brought our membership rolls up to date by the simple expedient of finding the name of a still-living member of the

25

church to go with every number reported. Also, this put us even further behind the brothers whose churches had gone in no directions but forward, onward, and upward, for while attendance at my church had increased, our membership had declined.

It was clear that something was wrong with my ministry. But where did the problem lie? In the preaching? In the pastoral care? In my femaleness? Finally I confessed my concern to a seminary professor.

"We have painted and carpeted, and one of the members arranged for new doors, but our membership hasn't doubled and neither has the budget. I have even been given a substantial raise, yet everyone else is doing so much better in terms of numbers and program than we are."

The professor grinned broadly. "I've been teaching here for ten years and I've heard all those stories hundreds of times. They are tall tales told to get the District Superintendent's attention and a bigger appointment."

"You mean they are not telling the truth?" I was horrified.

He laughed. "They're fighting for survival. You don't have to do that because you've got another job. Relax. Enjoy being a Methodist preacher."

I took the part of his advice that I could take. I am enjoying being a Methodist preacher, and my congregation seems to be enjoying it, too.

Toward the end of my fourth year as pastor at Wink, the chairperson of the administrative board brought a full-length mirror to install in my study. My mother watched me while I adjusted my robe and stole in front of it, and she said to the board chairperson, "You know, one of these days you'll have a male minister here, and with that flattering mirror you will never get him out of here to preach."

"Oh, no," the board chairperson assured her, "we don't want any male preachers here."

I smiled to myself as I recalled the words of the Episcopal priest who had shared a wedding with me in our church shortly after my appointment.

"Congregations will never accept women pastors," he had said. "Never."

"Perhaps not," I had replied. "But never is a long, long time."

II

The Vision Awaits Its Time

Mary Sue Gast

"It's really Roger we're interested in," explained Barbara Knapp, chairperson of the pastoral search committee of a United Church of Christ congregation in Michigan.

She and her husband had traveled from Union City, Michigan to Ames, Iowa where my husband, Roger Straw, and I were serving as campus ministers.

"Well," I replied, "we had hoped to share a pastorate."

"Or if only one of us can be hired, we want that one to be Mary Sue. I'd come along and see what might turn up for me," Roger added.

"You're certainly well-qualified, Mary Sue," Barbara hastened to say. "In fact, you're probably our strongest applicant. But our congregation's just not ready for a woman pastor."

"Let's talk about that," Roger and I replied.

And so the dialogue began one day in late February 1978.

Roger and I explained that it was currently more difficult for women to find placement as pastors, and for that reason we wanted to be sure that I had a call before we moved. We discussed how we apportion our work in a team ministry—

how for the first two months we both attend all functions and activities and then divide up responsibilities. We noted that they wouldn't be getting "two ministers for the price of one" if they hired us, but, as the Knapps were quick to point out, the congregation would get the benefit of two people's education, experience, skills, and perspectives.

Our conversation went on and on that afternoon. In that relaxed atmosphere we talked about Roger's and my different last names and why keeping them was important to us, helping us claim our individual identities as ministers; we talked about our hope to have children and share child-care responsibilities; we talked about small-town life and the needs of the congregation; and we concluded our time together by looking at pictures of the Knapps' grandchildren.

Bonds had been formed. As we progressed through the interview process that spring and the candidating sermons, we continued to make friends. The congregation's enthusiasm and openness to us sparked, and was sparked by, our excitement and interest in them. The call was extended to us as co-pastors. We accepted with joy.

Once again it seemed to be the case that a hypothetical woman minister was a lot more scary than a real one. Or, to put it another way, for a UCC clergywoman, the most difficult part in finding placement is getting a chance to meet with the Search Committee. My way was eased by the fact that I am married to a competent male minister who is more than willing to share a ministry with me and who is genuinely and generously supportive of my ministry. The Associate Conference Minister was also of great help; he actively put my Profile before Search Committees and assertively described my capabilities as a pastor. The congregation at Union City, after meeting me, was ready to take a giant step toward doing "a new thing" in its 141-year history.

But no change of this magnitude can come about totally without a hitch.

The Pastor Who's Married to the Pastor

There were, at first, some awkward moments when church people would introduce me as the minister's wife. Sometimes I let it pass, knowing that as I came before the congregation as preacher every other Sunday, as I worked with the boards and committees and community groups, the awareness would settle in that I, as well as Roger, was the pastor. More often, though, I would reach out to shake hands after such an introduction, adding in a friendly manner, "And I am also the minister."

Union City is a small town (1800 residents), situated at the union of two rivers amid the farmlands of Branch County in southwestern Michigan. First Congregational United Church of Christ is the second oldest of the eight congregations serving the community; with a membership of 250 it is one of the largest. People take their church life seriously here, and pastors are called upon to participate in the life of the village.

A number of church members feel that the former pastor at First Congregational was not extremely aggressive in his ministry, but almost everyone seems to agree that his wife was quite active in her ministry. Because of her, the congregation was accustomed to strong church leadership from a woman living in the parsonage.

There were some complications that arose from having as "predecessor" someone whose style of ministry was that of the "minister's wife." Many people assumed, at first, that I would fulfill that role, until it became more and more clear

30

that my professional duties would keep me from such involvements. For instance, several women's groups in town routinely extend membership to ministers' wives. I was pleased at the affection and warmth with which such invitations were issued, but at the same time I wondered whether anyone understood that I was bothered at being defined as "minister's wife" when that was not my primary calling. That question was answered for me one day as I stood talking with people after a planning meeting.

"Oh, Mary Sue, don't forget there's a Tuesday Club meeting this week."

I consulted my overburdened calendar. "It looks like I have something else going on then," I responded.

Then another woman remarked, "There's sure a lot of things going on for ministers' *wives* in this town. What about ministers' husbands?"

Her comment was oblique, but her facial expression and tone of voice were laden with meaning: Mary Sue can't be both the minister and the minister's wife. Those are two different jobs. She's our pastor. Don't expect her to be more than that. We don't ask Roger to be anything else besides the minister. The term "minister's wife" does mean something, and everytime you call Mary Sue "the minister's wife," you're ignoring the fact that she's the minister.

She understood my situation. Others were beginning to.

There have been members of the congregation who have grumbled that "the minister never came to call on me," when I, in fact, have called. In those cases I have been gratified to find churchwomen taking it upon themselves to inform the dissatisfied person that a call from Mary Sue is a call from the minister.

There have been painful incidents for me, such as when I found that a person with whom I had visited and prayed throughout the course of her final illness had specifically

31

requested that "the lady minister" not do her funeral. There have been times when I've been as confused as I am frustrated by ambiguous phone messages that make their way to the parsonage. When, for example, I am told that "the ministerial association is going to meet at 9 A.M. instead of 10 next week because the ladies of the host church would like to cook breakfast for 'the men,'" I cannot help but wonder whether I'm welcome for breakfast or not. But such happenings have occurred far less frequently than I had anticipated. For the most part I have experienced acceptance and love as a pastor.

Woman as Minister and Minister as Woman

I like to think that much of that acceptance and love I receive comes from the unique relationship that I, as Mary Sue Gast, human being, apart from gender, have with my congregation. But, given that Mary Sue Gast grew up female in this culture, perhaps some of that unique relationship is based on my being a woman.

I recall a children's story I told at worship one Sunday several months after arriving at Union City. I was intending to make the point that God is a Spirit and that maybe the best description we can give is that God is Love. In pursuit of that point I began by asking the children what God looks like. I was prepared to hear, "a man," and indeed that was the first answer given. But right on its heels came, "a woman." After the service several members of the congregation came up to me, smiling and saying with some wonder in their voices, "that never would have happened before you came here, Mary Sue."

So it may be that a woman minister in her symbolic role expands the definition of God, allows for new avenues in exploring who God is, and makes it possible for girls and

32

women to realize in a concrete way that they, too, are created in the image of God.

I know that my presence as a minister in Union City offers girls and young women (maybe some older women, too) new alternatives to consider when they're choosing their life's work. They may be moved to follow ministry as their calling or any number of other jobs that are meaningful and productive, even if these used to be considered as men's work. In the same way, the option of a man's doing housework and raising children is now visible in Roger. This is especially visible in premarital counseling and in the presentations we've made in the public schools. Our lifestyles have been valuable examples that open people up to fresh considerations about their own lives. I don't pressure anyone into choosing "my way," nor do I devalue other ways of living, but I believe that a choice freely made among many possibilities is stronger than a choice made with no reflection, within a limited framework.

My life is different from that of most of the people with whom and to whom I minister. The happy surprise has been that this has not been cause for alienation. I find I can bond with people who do farm, factory, office, or sales work and with those whose work is homemaking; as well as share the joys, griefs, worries, and appreciations that are part of the general human condition.

When I became pregnant, no one in the congregation voiced an assumption that I would cease or curtail my professional ministry after the baby was born. Susannah was born on July 20, 1979. I officiated at weddings throughout June, was in the pulpit July 15, led devotions at the Martha Circle July 19, and was in labor during a mission meeting on the 20th. I was not superwoman—the affliction euphemistically known as "morning sickness" virtually incapacitated me six hours a day for two months.

Fortunately I felt fine at 11 A.M., and was able to juggle meeting times and to use many of my hours of recumbency for studying, phone calls, and planning. The congregation accommodated to the whole process with seeming delight. And I judged we were in a new stage of openness with one another one spring day in 1979 as a number of women stood around the kitchen after a meeting. The case of a firefighter in Iowa who was nursing her baby while on duty had been receiving a lot of news coverage. The president of the Women's Fellowship referred to that news item and then turned to me and asked, "Are you going to nurse your baby in the pulpit?" A great time of laughter and personal sharing followed.

A woman as pastor brings new dimensions to ministry. Maybe more important, having a pastor who is a woman makes it necessary for a congregation to question many deeply held presuppositions about ministers and ministry. From matters of attire to images of authority, clergywomen, by our very presence, call presuppositions into question. Clergywomen don't automatically dress in dark suits and ties; even in clerical collars we don't "look like" ministers to most people—at first. We don't evoke those unconscious images of Authority, as portrayed by Charleton Heston. Yet each clergywoman has her own authority, no matter how soft-spoken, or small of stature, or (heaven help us), "cute" she may be.

As time passes, the congregation served by a clergy-woman sees that the question isn't, "Does she look like a minister?" Instead the realization grows that there is no single mold of ministry to be filled. The realization expands to include the awareness that all followers of Christ wear the face of ministry; ministry looks like each of us. Likewise, in matters of authority, the congregation finds that true authority lies within a person and expresses itself uniquely

34

in each one. It may be quiet or dramatic, boisterous or calm, but it's there. In learning to see and hear authority in this new pastor, the congregation is opened up to looking for authority in each other, in themselves.

So we find that the process of questioning the previously unspoken presuppositions results in a sifting out of the marginal characteristics from the central issues of ministry. The congregation gains in the understanding of ministry and more members are enabled to claim their own ministry.

"I've Never Heard a Woman Preach . . ."

People have asked me, "Do you preach women's liberation?" The answer I give is, "I preach the gospel." Yet I know that I preach in a particular way because I am a woman who is conscious that injustice and limitation have characterized women's and men's roles for, literally, ages. My language includes references to both women and men; my sermon illustrations feature people of both sexes in roles that are not the overdone caricatures of nagging wife, blundering father, coy sister, etc.; I honor and include experiences common to women and to men. When I prepare a sermon, I first complete the appropriate academic and historical study so that I will be true to the meaning of the text. Then I actively set aside all the familiar buildup of interpretation and application a given passage is laden with. I want the Word to hit me in new ways. I work at understanding each character involved in a biblical narrative. I reread the dialogues with different voices. I restage the drama until something fresh and true resounds through it for me. So I come up with Abraham, in the manner of a seven-year-old, pleading with God not to destroy Sodom, while God is standing in the kitchen stirring the spaghetti sauce. Jesus has come across as Fonzie to Peter's Richie

35

Cunningham. At those times my congregation feels new recognition of the dynamics at work between God and Abraham, between Jesus and Peter. Out of that sense of recognition there is born a readiness to receive the Word with openness to the very real costs and joys of discipleship.

"I feel so *included* in what you say," I've been told. I treasure that. "You sure do make the Bible real," is another way it's put—by both women and men. I feel like I'm doing my job well at those times.

The Vision Coming Clearer

Union City has had a woman as pastor since mid-1978. The church building has not been threatened by judgmental lightning bolts, the marriages solemnized have been accepted by the State of Michigan, new members have joined, old members have stayed active. Changes in structure have occurred, and some of those changes were, no doubt, first considered because a woman was serving as pastor. One example of these changes can be found in the Boards of Deacons and Deaconesses. We had studied together the biblical background of the Diaconate, and the time came when we had to write up a description of roles and duties for the updating of the bylaws. There was general agreement that "esses" should be dropped, and all members should be called deacons. There was the briefest of silences before someone said, "Well, if we all have the same title we probably should all do the same jobs." Agreed. It was one of the male deacons who then took up the implicit challenge. "I'll cut up the bread for communion next Sunday. Minard, why don't you help me?"

On the first Sunday of 1980, communion was served by three men and one woman, a woman who, at the Deacons' meeting, had articulated her concern that men continue to

36

serve the church in visible and important ways while at the same time women be free to minister in all areas of church life. There were tears in my eyes during the Lord's Supper at the beauty of it. A more complete human community was represented. I felt a warmth on the cold edge of a loneliness I'd not even been aware of. I was no longer the only woman embodying spiritual leadership for this congregation.

In May of 1979 the Church Council was meeting to discuss and state views on the resolutions that were to come before the Annual Meeting of the Michigan Conference UCC. As we made our way through the tangle of controversial topics we came upon one resolution asking that congregations demonstrate an openness to calling women to be pastors. The atmosphere lightened as a Trustee said, "I guess we can all go along with this one." As unanimity was expressed, one of the delegates to the Annual Meeting chuckled. "I can hardly wait to hassle the delegates from those big churches in Detroit and Grand Rapids," he said. "There they are, waiting around, while we go ahead and call a woman pastor. They don't know what they're missing."

Before I came to Union City I didn't know what I was missing either.

(In the Spring of 1981 Mary Sue Gast and her husband, Roger Straw, left Union City to accept a call to Grand Rapids. The congregation called a woman as the minister to succeed Mary Sue and Roger.)

III

The Anatomy of a Call

Ansley Coe Throckmorton

To Dorothy L. Watt, Clerk of Hammond Street Congregational Church Corporation:

You are hereby requested to notify and warn the members of said Corporation to meet in the Sanctuary of their meeting house on Sunday, December 10, 1978 at 11:15 A.M.

To consider and act upon the recommendation of the Pulpit Committee that Ansley Coe Throckmorton be called as the Senior Minister of Hammond Street Congregational Church.

To transact such other and further business as may legally come before the meeting.

And you are hereby requested to make a return of this Warrant with your doings thereon on or before the date of said meeting.

Given by order of the Church Council this 29th day of November, 1978.

Perham L. Amsden
Moderator, Hammond Street
Congregational Church Corporation

Behind that correct and straightforward official letter lies a church that is uniquely of our time. A local church was about to call a woman to be its minister. On December 10, 1978 the Hammond Street Congregational Church, United Church of Christ, a predominantly white congregation of nearly five hundred members, in Bangor, Maine, did call me to be its senior minister. This call could not have happened in 1970 any place in this country except as an anomaly. That it could happen as it did in 1978 illustrates the dramatic changes of the 1970s with regard to the ministry of women and the openness of churches to them.

Questions are posed with regard to such changes. What kind of congregation would consider calling a woman as senior minister? What kind of ecclesiastical polity would encourage this? What kind of women would be ready to respond? In short the story of my call by that church to be its minister can be told as the story of a parish, a polity and a person called to the ministry. These three coincided at the right time in history and something new happened. This chapter tells that story.

I. The Parish

The Hammond Street Congregational Church was founded in 1833. Throughout its nearly one-hundred-and-fifty-year history, it has had a tradition of supporting world missions, local mission, seminary education and the education of its members. In short, it is a church in which the gospel is not stillborn, but rather issues forth in witness and service by its members. This is significant in the present story. Churches that are primarily turned in on themselves approach what is new with fear. Hammond Street Church turns out to the world. Historically its leadership has had the faith and vision to focus on the gospel and not on the

39

church itself. The result has been an openness to the spirit through which new things have been possible.

Another characteristic of the church that affected the course of events is the heterogeneity of its membership. Among the faithful five hundred are people of all ages and professions and of varied educational, economic, ethnic, and cultural backgrounds and circumstances. It is inherently an open parish, ripe for new ventures.

Hindsight, with its perfect vision, would indicate that this was a church ready for whatever change was necessary. Blessed by its heterogeneous, inclusive membership, having deep roots in the past, yet not threatened by change, having strong lay leadership and a long tradition of enlightened clergy leadership, and having had a woman associate minister, it was open to new light and new directions. When the first wave of ordained women came on the scene in the mid-twentieth century, it was ready.

I was invited in 1972 to be the Director of Religious Education. In 1973 I was ordained. In 1975, with the coming of a new senior minister, Peter Mercer, I was made the Associate Minister. Three years later, when he left, I assumed I would be leaving too. I could not become the associate to a third minister in the church and I had been offered another attractive position I was prepared to accept.

The pulpit committee meanwhile, having canvassed the church rather carefully, decided that I would be considered a candidate for the position of senior minister. I was invited to meet with them, and in the end they voted to recommend me to the membership, which, in turn, voted to call me to be the minister of the church. I accepted and we have moved ahead without doubt, hesitation, or regret to our life together of witness and service.

I am often asked if there was opposition along the way.

"Were you rejected?" "Did you encounter resistance?" "Were there ugly incidents or hurtful remarks?" I am reluctant to discuss such questions. After nearly nine years at Hammond Street Church, my gender is now, practically speaking, a nonissue. Of course it wasn't always so. That I am a woman had to be a problem to some and needed to be thought through by others in the church. Could I carry the load? Did I preach well enough? Could I be heard? Was I qualified for this particular church? Would my sex alienate people? The questions had to be answered. It wasn't easy for anyone.

There had been a woman associate minister in the church before me. That helped some. But no woman in our culture can pave the way for another. Not yet. The real burden on us all in a historically male profession is that each woman must make her own way and each church is also breaking new ground. We were no exception.

It would be naïve to suppose that twenty centuries of Christian history, overwhelmingly biased against the ordination of women, could be routinely swept aside even by the enormous good will of the people I serve. Nor, for that matter, could I, even with my sure sense of calling, sweep it all away in my own mind. Centuries of doubt about women in the ministry have left their mark on us all. We made our way together with growing trust and confidence. I respected the intentions and wisdom of my people. I learned to be patient with the progress we made together. In the end, trust and mutual strength grew from our life together in Christ.

A particular parish was the opportunity.

II. The Polity

Free church polity directed the process leading to my becoming the minister of the Hammond Street Church.

41

Though we in the United Church of Christ have the assistance and counsel of Conference Ministers available to us, the responsibility for discerning the "right" person for a particular parish rests with its members. No bishop, district superintendent, or presbytery can make that decision. The members of the church, under the guidance of the Holy Spirit, must decide on the recommendation of a pulpit committee, which has been similarly guided.

Hammond Street Church, throughout its history, has been "congregational." The governing unit of its life and order is the congregation. There is no earthly power external to it that can determine its life, its worship, or its ministry. While we live in a covenant relationship with other churches, we are, as we love to say, autonomous. This form of church government has large implications for the ministry of women—some helpful and some not helpful. As for the latter, for example, while a bishop might appoint a woman or a black to a reluctant church, thereby circumventing prejudice and accelerating the transforming of attitudes, that appointment might also stir up enough anger to bring untold suffering on the minister and the church—a situation that exists far too often. With congregational polity, however, change may come slowly, but when it comes by the sacred vote of the people it may come without resentment and with profound and effective conviction.

On more than one occasion my position as a minister of this church was submitted to a vote of the membership. Each time, for a number of reasons, the atmosphere was charged and the ballot was a secret written one. The most recent vote, when I was called to be the senior minister, resulted in a vote clearly in favor of calling me. But it was not without significant opposition. I look on the unanimous or near unanimous calls of my male colleagues in the ministry with amazement. But who needs it? Churches need, for strength, a membership committed to the person of Jesus Christ, not primarily to the minister. It is the ultimate tribute to the people of my church that, once it was decided, they were and are united. Very, very few turned away. Some who probably opposed my election went out of their way to indicate their intention to be faithful to their church and to support me in my responsibilities. That is "congregational" polity at its best.

III. The Women Called to the Ministry

What of the woman who would be ready to respond to that call? Much of the answer to that question may be read between the lines of the preceding pages. More will have to be told by others who are more objective. For my part of the answer some observations are in order.

Dorothy Sayers once made this comment: "I am occasionally desired by congenital imbeciles and the editors of magazines to say something about the writing of detective fiction 'from the woman's point of view.' To such demands, one can only say, 'Go away and don't be silly.' You might as well ask what is the female angle on an equilateral triangle."

Dorothy Sayers' observation is partly true (but only partly) with regard to the ministry. When we become *preoccupied* with role identity and "gender mystiques" and "sexual stereotypes" in reference to the ministry, we are in serious trouble. We must not succumb to the pathetic fallacy and distortion that the ministry can be described or defined with reference to sexual characteristics. That was the error of the church for nineteen centuries. It is time that it ended. Unless and until we are, all of us, male and female,

43

grounded and immersed in a biblical perspective that is timeless and universal and that does not attempt to bind the Holy Spirit, we are tragically out of touch with the only reason for the existence of the ministry.

What are the biblical images for the ministry? Those who are sent are called "servants" of Jesus Christ, "ambassadors," "earthen vessels," "builders," "planters" "public spectacles" where God's action takes place. What do sexual characteristics have to do with any of these? That maleness should have become a matter of surpassing importance is a gross distortion of the church's ministry, whose biblical claim is that all this is from God, that God's grace is sufficient, and that God's power is made perfect in weakness, without respect to gender.

In a sense, however, Dorothy Sayers' observation does not apply to the ministry as we have known it, for the very reason that the church has had a male ministry throughout its existence until only recently. That being the case, any change in practice needs to name the cultural error and consciously find ways not only to correct the long practice of a strictly male clergy, but to avoid an equally unbiblical "female" clergy. Obedience to Jesus Christ requires the renunciation of centuries of sex-role stereotyping and of recent polarization as well. Rosemary Ruether has said the essence of the ministry transcends and overcomes both. Some conscious and self-conscious effort will be necessary in the church for some time to come. It can and must be done.

In short, I was prepared to succeed twelve male ministers of Hammond Street Church because I was not locked into a stereotyped understanding of the ministry or of myself, but rather was instructed by the biblical images of the ministry. Furthermore, I was compelled by a force I could not resist and freed by a spirit and energy I had not known to obey the dictates of my calling. In every respect—in preaching, pastoral care, and administration—the practice of 147 years in my parish and of 19 centuries in the church was no longer binding.

IV. Conclusion

There are some advantages to being "different" in terms of the long practice of a solely male clergy—advantages that are at the same time amusing and instructive. One of these is that women are mercifully free of being identified with the sanctimonious caricature of the male clergy, which is a commonplace in cartoons, on television, and in daily conversation. Another advantage is that a woman occupying the senior position on a staff need never play the role of the "boss" over others. She is naturally emancipated to evolve, with her colleagues, working relationships that depend more on gifts and responsibilities than on authority.

These are plusses. But the real plus that overrides all others and is available to female and male alike is the grace of God. No matter what the inadequacies of our personal lives or of our cultural limitations, it is God who will empower any particular ministry. I must speak very personally of this. As a woman I have, on occasion, been put down, left out, or passed by. But women in the ministry don't have a corner on hardship or rejection. While I have known difficult times in my ministry, I can also say that I have been forgiven, healed, restored, lifted up, inspired, and filled with joy and peace in believing. God's grace has been sufficient for me and I know that God's power will be made perfect in my weakness, for as it was in the beginning, it is now and it always shall be.

IV

A Call to a Co-pastorate

Anne Rosser

"Does she really comprehend the awful implication of her resolution? How in the name of all that is holy and righteous can she proclaim that women are subordinate to men—that they were created for passive, subservient roles in society? If the lifestyle of the Christian—male, as well as female—is that of servanthood, where in the world did the perversion of this teaching arise, in that throughout the history of the Christian Church, woman has been cast into the servant role while man has assumed the role of master?"

Such were the questions racing through my mind as I listened to a pastor's wife from Texas read a resolution opposing women's liberation at the annual meeting of the Southern Baptist Convention in Portland, Oregon, in mid-June, 1973. Mrs. Smith (not her real name) based her statement upon her interpretation of I Corinthians 11:3, 8-9. She considered the modern women's movement as a travesty of, indeed, almost a blasphemy against, God's will and purpose for humanity. As I struggled inwardly with mingled feelings of anger, despair, and frustration, Mrs. Smith continued with her legalistic misinterpretation of the Scripture.

Traditionally, Southern Baptists, as a denomination, have tended neither to the far left or right theologically. The great silent majority of us have simply drifted along in midstream as theological moderates. In the 1973 meeting, however, a decided shift to the far right was observed as the convention in business session overwhelmingly approved Mrs. Smith's resolution.

In our church in Richmond at that time, I was the pastor's wife and the teacher of a large Sunday school class of older, mature women. A great deal of my teaching had to do with consciousness-raising, for many of the women in our church had no real sense of identity apart from their husband and/or children. I had worked through some of the more difficult passages in the New Testament epistles with the class members, using commentaries from the library of our nearby college.

After returning home from Portland, my husband, Buddy, and I continued to discuss the issue and to raise questions that begged for answers: (1) Why have women throughout church history, much less Southern Baptist history, been excluded from meaningful service in the church? (2) How did the exclusion of women as pastors and preachers come about? (3) If, indeed, the biblical revelation affirmed women as created in the image of God and thus equal to men in every respect, how could we in our work in the local church implement and actualize this basic truth?

One morning at breakfast, Buddy raised the question: "Why don't you consider the possibility of going back to school, even seminary, for graduate study?" He seemed to feel instinctively that I needed an opportunity to enlarge my own horizons as well as explore for solutions and answers to the pressing issue of women's role in church and society.

Approximately two weeks later, I applied for admission

to Union Theological Seminary in Virginia. The Admissions Committee very graciously accepted me.

New students at Union Seminary spend the short September quarter in a basic course: "Introduction to Ministry." Taught by a team of faculty members as well as by a working pastor in a local Presbyterian church, the course opened up, quite extraordinarily, a whole new world for me. One of the teachers, Dr. J. A. Ross Mackenzie, Professor of Church History, took special pains to make the women students feel at home in the seminary setting. In one of his presentations before the class, he affirmed the gospel tradition in the early church where women were fully recognized as spiritual leaders. Yes, along with men, they became preachers, teachers, evangelists, and missionaries. Indeed, one of the most prominent traditions in all four gospels is the fact that the women disciples were the first to find the tomb of Jesus empty. Both Mark and Luke proclaim that the news of Jesus' resurrection was first given to women. Matthew and John reveal that the risen Jesus first appeared to women (miracle of miracles—in John He appears first to one woman alone, Mary Magdalene). All four gospel traditions inform us that the women disciples were the first Christian preachers, for they were commissioned to tell Peter and the other apostles the basic teaching of Christianity: Jesus is alive—he is risen!

In the September quarter of my second year, Dr. Mackenzie taught a course provocatively titled "Keeping Women in Their Place: Mary and Woman in the Church." It was open, of course, to both men and women students. It proved to be the watershed in my seminary study. Under Dr. Mackenzie's inspired teaching (his bibliography included a rich collection of resource books, periodicals, and audio-visual presentations from the seminary library) I became aware that God might be calling me into the pastoral ministry. In my outside reading for the course, I came across a most enlightening article in the field of biblical studies. Amazingly, the author was a female theologian from my own tradition, Dr. Phyllis Trible. Her article appeared in the Andover-Newton Seminary Quarterly for March, 1973 (pp. 251-257). She now serves as Professor of Hebrew and Old Testament Interpretation at Union Theological Seminary in New York.

Dr. Trible points out in "Eve and Adam: Genesis 2-3 Reread" that the Hebrew word NEGED in Genesis 2:18 implies equality. (It is translated "fit" in RSV.) The male needed a counterpart, or "helper" in the sense of "equal partner," "fit" for him. "Helper" in this context carries no note of inferiority, for the same Hebrew word is used in various other biblical references to indicate God's "help." Trible states (p. 252) "God is the helper superior to man; the animals are helpers inferior to man; but woman is the helper *equal* to man." In depicting woman as the last of creation, the Yahwistic writer in Genesis reveals that he sees her as the culmination of creation, *not* as a weak anticlimax (v. 22). The concept of "bone of my bones" and "flesh of my flesh" (v. 23) denotes the oneness and inclusiveness of sexual union; it expresses deep, caring love, loyalty, and responsibility—never subordination. Indeed, Dr. Trible's brilliant exegetical studies have rendered obsolete most commentaries on Genesis published prior to 1970.

Another subject of inestimable value in my seminary curriculum was the second-year theology course dealing with Christology. Dr. Donald G. Dawe helped tremendously in enlarging our understanding of what God was about in the person of Jesus Christ. My project for the Christology course involved writing a paper of critical reflection on Karl Barth's matchless exposition on the Virgin birth, "The Miracle of Christmas." Barth proclaims that "In

Jesus Christ, God comes forth out of the profound hiddenness of His divinity in order to act as God among us and upon us." Like that of Dr. Mackenzie, Dr. Dawe's teaching had an inspirational quality that encouraged his students to dig more deeply into the mystery and wisdom of the biblical revelation. Indeed, as I began to read more widely in the fields of church history and theology, the burning questions that propelled me to seek seminary training in the first place were resolved most thoroughly and profoundly.

My Student-in-Ministry year, as part of the Doctor of Ministry curriculum, was arranged to be spent in the nearby Ginter Park Baptist Church, with the minister, Dr. Elmer S. West, serving as my pastor/advisor. This assignment was especially meaningful to me because Ginter Park Baptist was the church in which I had been nurtured and reared. My major task there was to begin a ministry to the senior citizens. As the year unfolded, we saw the formation of an energetic and fun-loving group of seniors who called themselves the "39-ers" (39 years and holding!). I felt especially close to these wonderful people, for I had known most of them since my early childhood. I am convinced that my year as a student-in-ministry served to solidify and confirm my call to the pastoral ministry. One of the highlights of the year was the ordination of the first women deacons in the history of Ginter Park Baptist Church. They were well received and affirmed by most of the congregation. A great deal of the credit for this is due to Dr. West's own sensitive and caring attitude toward all people.

Another friend and mentor was Dr. Sarah Little, Union Seminary's first woman professor. Eminently qualified to teach both preachers and teachers, she was very supportive of women in ministry and gave unstintingly and sacrificially of her time and counsel.

In preparation for my ordination service on June 4, 1978, I searched through the manuals of several denominations in the files of the seminary library. Uppermost in our concern for the service was that it must be primarily a service of worship, reflecting those commonly held convictions and teachings shared by all faithful followers of Jesus Christ. My call, like that of my husband's, was to the ministry of the gospel, not to any narrow, sectarian doctrinal stance. In my research I was relieved to discover that most Baptist ordination documents were comparatively free of hard-line parochialism and fundamentalism. The manual I finally found to be in accord with our own concept of ministry was the one used by British Baptists today. Traditional in its language and theology, it nevertheless reflects an openness to the future. What impressed me a great deal is that the foreword to the document actually states that women as well as men are called to the gospel ministry, and, therefore, the service material can be used for either a woman's or a man's ordination ceremony.

The ordination service was held on June 4, 1978. My husband, as well as our four sons, Aubrey, Stephen, Philip, Jonathan, and our daughter-in-law, Donna, had been lovingly supportive of me all the way through the educational process. Donna was the organist for the service. Aubrey (her husband and our oldest son) prayed the ordination prayer. Stephen, our second son, directed the choir in the anthem, and sang the tenor aria "Then Shall the Righteous Shine Forth" from Mendelssohn's "Elijah" Oratorio. Philip, our third son, read the Old Testament reading (Isaiah 6:1-8). Jonathan, our fourth son, read from the New Testament (II Corinthians 4:5-18).

The euphoria and feeling of blessing and fulfillment accompanying the ordination event helped buoy me through the next eight months of searching and waiting for a place to serve. We had hoped to minister together as a team in the church Buddy served as pastor and in which I was ordained. Regrettably, feelings against women in ministry ran strong and deep throughout the congregation. Amazingly, the opposition to women in ministry cut across all economic and occupational lines of our people. On the surface, what appeared to be theological reasons for denying women leadership roles in ministry actually boiled down to emotional reactions against the blurring of cultural roles and expectations. However, I remember feeling especially proud of several of our members who had not had the good fortune of obtaining an extensive formal education, and yet, by the grace of God, had remained open and receptive through the years to the work of God in their midst. These people assured me of their love and support, offering to help in any way they could. Sadly, others with fine educational advantages were unable to accept my changed status as a minister. Quite frankly, they seemed to feel I would become a threat to them.

From June, 1978, to April, 1979, Buddy and I wrote and/or visited many people in leadership positions of our own denomination as well as those of the United Methodist, Presbyterian, and Disciples of Christ churches. In the midst of uncertainty about my future in ministry, I found great comfort in the conviction (certain knowledge) that God, who had brought me this far, was not about to abandon me.

And then, one night in late March, 1979, our phone rang at home. The caller identified himself as Dr. Harold Greer, co-chairman of the pulpit committee of the Bainbridge-Southampton Baptist Church in South Richmond. He had heard me speak to the students at a recent meeting of the Baptist Student Union on the campus of Virginia Commonwealth University in downtown Richmond. He was Professor of History at the University and also served as an advisor to the BSU. He knew that Buddy and I were hoping to minister as a team someday, and he expressed great interest in this possibility. He asked if we could meet with him and Mr. Alfred Lewis, the other co-chairman of the pulpit committee, in his home. We agreed. In the time of sharing with these two conscientious, dedicated men, my husband and I felt a sense of peace and well-being. Both men were leaders in their church—a church known as one congregation with two locations. One location was in the inner city of Richmond at Eleventh and Bainbridge Streets. The other was in the suburbs of the city at Cherokee and Chellowe Roads.

Through our meetings, again with the co-chairmen, and then later with the full pulpit committee, we began to feel a sense of call, an identification with these people who shared so many concerns with us. And so it was arranged for the congregation to meet in business session following family night supper on Wednesday night, July 18, 1979, to consider calling us as co-pastors.

Following our presentation to the congregation, Buddy and I waited in the pastor's study. After a while, word came that the vote to call us as co-pastors had been unanimous. Voting was done by secret ballot. We were overjoyed at the news, and, at the same time, overwhelmed that God should confirm his call to us to serve as a team in such a totally affirming way. A unanimous vote by secret ballot is extremely rare in Baptist meetings!

On Sunday night, September 9, 1979, we were formally installed as co-pastors of the Bainbridge-Southampton Baptist Church in a worship service held in the Bainbridge sanctuary. The charge to us as the new pastors was brought by our dear friend of many years' standing, Dr. Theodore F. Adams, Pastor Emeritus of Richmond's First Baptist Church and former President of the Baptist World Alliance. The charge to the church was brought by another dear friend, Dr. Elmer West.

After two years in our joint ministry with the Bainbridge-Southampton Baptist Church, my husband and I are convinced that all of our previous work and experiences in past pastorates have been preparation for this very strategic place of service. It is strategic for at least two reasons. (1) Our congregation is attempting to combine a traditional suburban ministry with a transitional ministry in the inner city. (2) In calling a female pastor to serve on an equal level, not on a subordinate one, with a male pastor, this congregation is affirming the divine intent at creation when God created human beings, both male and female, in the image of God. "And God blessed them. . . ." (See exegesis of Genesis 2 above.) We receive equal salary checks each month, and all fringe benefits are equal. We feel that our church is teaching, albeit subliminally, that God is imaged as both male and female.

In our discussions with the pulpit committee prior to our coming, we felt that it would be better for us to exchange pulpits each Sunday morning, rather than every month or two. This would enable the people to become acquainted with both of us more quickly. Our Sunday evening services are always held together at one location—for the past year now at the Southampton location. Our Wednesday evening family night suppers and mission meetings are held together, alternating from one location to the other each week.

One of the most remarkable, and at the same time humbling, aspects of my call to serve as a minister of the gospel has been the heightened awareness within me of what God was about in the person of Jesus Christ, particularly as I have celebrated the ordinances of baptism and the Lord's Supper with our congregation. We celebrate the Eucharist, or Lord's Supper, on the first Sunday morning of each month at both locations.

Our first baptismal service was held on Sunday morning, June 1, 1980, with the congregation united at one location (Bainbridge). We felt we should do this together since it was the first time a woman pastor had ever baptized candidates in a Southern Baptist church. I baptized Carolyn Moss Riddle, and Buddy baptized her husband, Rhett. Then I baptized Jimmy Barbour and R. W. Nuckols, and Buddy baptized Fay Collier. There is, of course, no magic or saving efficacy in the ordinances. However, what they portray about God and God's limitless love for us is inexpressible through the medium of words alone. As long as I live I shall never forget the radiant, life-affirming expressions on the faces of these dear friends, the first people I baptized.

"How great is the grace of God, which has been given to us in such large measure!"

V

What Do We Call You?

Maribeth Blackman-Sexton

There were three of us seated in the family room, talking about the weather, then the grandchildren, and finally the church. As we talked about the church, the subject of former pastors became our focus. The two long-time members sat across from me and talked about "Brother So-and-So" who had served several years earlier; "Brother So-and-So" who had only stayed a few months; and "Brother So-and-So," the pastor who had served part-time while finishing a seminary career. Suddenly the woman smiled, looked at me quizzically and asked, "What do we call you?" It was a question I would hear many times as I made my first calls in my first full-time pastorate in the county seat of Cotton County, Oklahoma.

It probably is not easy being the first church in a small, rural, conservative community to call a woman as pastor. (Long after my arrival, some of the members reported to me that they had been questioned, then criticized by many of their friends in the community because they belonged to the church that had hired "that woman" to be their pastor.) Small wonder, then, that there was some hesitation at first; some question about how to address this unknown being, "the lady preacher." There was also a period of trial and testing. Can she really preach? For several Sundays in the beginning of my ministry with my current church, there were larger-than-average crowds in attendance at our Sunday morning worship services who wanted to see if I really could preach.

Throughout the entire process of our getting to know one another, however, I always felt that, despite whatever troublesome issues my presence might raise, I was loved and accepted. Once the congregation decided to extend a call to me, they were willing to risk whatever results that call might bring. One result was that two families left the church.

First Christian Church and I have been "married" now for four years. During that time, we have made several discoveries about each other. They have discovered their minister's "wife" (who is actually a husband) can bake a fairly reputable batch of cookies for the parsonage open house. They have discovered their minister is stronger than she looks—that she can baptize a full-grown adult male (by immersion) without even flinching. They have discovered that, although their minister has a soprano voice, she can be heard on the back row without a microphone. After I had preached several sermons in this church, an elderly woman with a hearing problem came up to me after services one day, shook my hand, smiled, and said, "Usually I can't hear but about half of the sermon, but when you preach, I don't have any trouble hearing you."

I have discovered a sense of excitement among our members. They are trying something new—something that no other church in this farming community has tried—and something that gives them a unique identity. "We're the church with the lady preacher." I have discovered that, although they as a church, and I as the pastor of that church, have been denounced in some of the other local pulpits, there is a tremendous feeling of pride and "family" unity among us. While there may be those within the church who still have questions concerning the theological okay-ness of a woman pastor, any hint from outside that we might be less than acceptable in God's eyes has met strong resistance and has served to solidify our relationship.

Lots of the concerns and questions formerly asked about women pastors are no longer issues. Questions that used to be raised in pulpit committee interviews dealt with lots of "what if's." What if she gets married? What if she gets pregnant? When I first entered the ministry as a weekend youth minister, I was a newlywed. I entered that ministry with the full support of my husband. He is still one of my most avid supporters, currently serving as an elder and a Sunday school teacher (by his own choice and at their request, not demand). People are still curious about how our two-career relationship functions, but he is no longer regarded as a threat—as someone who will one day take their minister away. Furthermore, it seems no one would be the least offended if this minister's "wife" decided to pursue a career outside the church and parsonage.

While I was serving as a student pastor in another community, we dealt with the issue of pregnancy in the pulpit. Shortly after accepting that call, I discovered that I was pregnant. After the church made that same discovery, one of the older members asked another, "What do you suppose she'll do now?" The other replied, "I suppose she'll have a baby in a few months." At our monthly fellowship supper, I shared our good news with the congregation. I simply announced that I planned to continue as their pastor; that I would need perhaps two weeks to recuperate after the baby was born, and that I anticipated no problems in continuing beyond that. When the pregnancy became a little more obvious, I began to wear a robe. The "disguise" must have worked very well, because on Sunday morning as I greeted the worshipers after church, a gentleman who had just moved back into the community said, as he shook my hand, "You know, when we first got back to town and learned that the Christian Church had a woman pastor, I had some reservations. But once you got up in the pulpit and began to preach, I did not even notice that you were a woman." I was doubly flattered. Not only had he indirectly complimented my sermon, but I was eight months pregnant and he did not notice I was a woman!

There are other issues that have not been so easily resolved. For example, there is the occasional sense of isolation that I, as a woman pastor in a community of male clergy, sometimes experience. While many of my male colleagues are supportive of my ministry, I am not "one of the guys." I am active in our local ministerial alliance (although I have turned down two requests to serve as secretary of that organization), but I am not invited to join the other ministers when they get together for an informal game of golf. As professionals in ministry, we have some common concerns, but as a woman in the church I have more in common with their wives at times. Therefore, it is difficult to form close friendships with either group.

I hope that, as the number of women entering the pastoral ministry increases, isolation will also cease to be a problem. In our denomination, as in several others, more women are entering seminary with the intention of becoming pastors. The Disciples of Christ have a full-time general staff person who coordinates communication among women pastors and provides support/nurture events for us.

There is also the issue of an intrapersonal conflict

59

between my own feminist philosophy and activism and the limits pastoral caring sets on that. In other words, out of fear and love, I am not always the prophet for equality that I would like to be. There is genuine fear that I would lose my job, but there is also genuine love for the people I serve. I would not want to alienate those whom I have been called to love.

Being a woman in the ministry of a local congregation is funny. It is sad. It is also exciting. It is funny when someone asks one of my church members, "How do you like your lady preacher?" and he replies, "I don't know how the women feel, but the men sure like her." It is funny when I am introduced by a church member to one of their friends as "my pastor," and that friend stares at me with open mouth and eyes before recovering enough to say something.

It is sad when I receive a telephone call in the middle of the night from someone needing help, who would rather hang up than trust the counseling skills of a woman. It is sad when I must prove my professional status by showing my minister's identification card, in order to make a pastoral call to a critically ill member in the intensive care unit of a hospital. It is sad when someone who has never set foot in my church says to me, "I just cannot see having a woman as a preacher."

Above all, however, this crazy career I have chosen is exciting. It is exciting to be on the cutting edge of a growing movement. It is exciting to walk into the pulpit on Sunday morning and know that I belong there. It is exciting to be part of a group that seeks to make more visible, within the community of the faithful, the feminine half of the divine image. It is exciting when "Mrs. Smith," an elderly member of a more conservative church in our community, can say to me following a service in which we participated together, "The more I hear you, the more I am convinced that a woman can do anything." Not every person I come into contact with is so easily convinced, but I do see changes taking place in people's attitudes and responsiveness.

One day, three-year-old Christy, the daughter of one of our members, rode down the street and passed one of our sister churches with whom we share a vacation church school program. Christy was talking with her mother about the Bible school she had attended there. Then they began to talk about church in general. As they talked, Christy told her mother, "I think I'll be a preacher when I grow up." When Christy's grandmother told me the story, we agreed that if Christy had been born as recently as ten years ago, she probably would never have thought of that. If my presence as her pastor has opened that door of possibility for Christy, then that *is* exciting.

"What do we call you?" The question may be with us for yet a little while, until "Sister So-and-So's" become as numerous and traditional as "Brother So-and-So's" have been. In my brief career, I have found that it does not matter so much *what* I am called as it matters *that* I am called. When I listen to someone's pain, I am called pastor. When I proclaim the Good News, I am called preacher. When I become involved in the issues of our day, I am called prophet.

It was not long ago that Andrew, an elder in our church, came to me one day, all excited and happy about a conversation he had had with another minister. Unbeknownst to me he had been concerned about some of the criticism he had heard, which said that women *were not* ordained in God's eyes. The other minister had shared with him the twentieth chapter of the gospel of John, verses 17 and 18: "Jesus said to her, 'Do not hold me, for I have not yet ascended to the Father; but go to my brethren and say to them, I am ascending to my Father and your Father, to my

61

God and your God.' Mary Magdalene went and said to the disciples, 'I have seen the Lord,' and she told them that he had said these things to her." Andrew smiled. "According to that, Jesus directly commissioned a woman to preach the gospel. That means you are ordained and that it's okay for us to have a woman preacher." That's why I entered the ministry, Andrew. I am glad that I have been called by a congregation to serve as pastor. But, more important, I have been called by Christ, and that is one call neither I nor the church can ignore.

VI

The Long Road

Ellen Brubaker

She seemed smaller than usual, lying there in her hospital bed. I could hear her speaking into the telephone, saying words that no one wanted to hear. More surgery was necessary, she was saying, they hadn't got it all the first time. My tears came unbidden. Why? Why this for Marjorie? Why now? Why ever to this woman of courage so needed in ministry? It wasn't fair! She had already come through far more than her share of struggles. When does the strength of one human being come to an end?

We cried together. Marjorie cried first of all because she is a human being, a child of God, full of life. Cancer was a threat to her life and to her ministry. Yet this struggle, as all other struggles, joys, sorrows, victories, and defeats, was soon put where she puts her total life—in God's hands.

Her second concern during that illness was the frustration of her driving purpose for ministry. She had walked a long road into the ordained ministry of The United Methodist Church and had many miles yet to walk. Limitations were not her style.

She cried too for us, we women in ministry who had come

to depend on her for guidance and inspiration. "I don't want to let you down," she said that day. She hasn't. She won't.

Marjorie Swank Matthews has never been in the business of letting people down. The year she entered the ministry, the U. S. Labor Department listed 270 women as clergy. The following year the number had dwindled to 243. Obstacles to women pastors were greater then in The United Methodist Church. But obstacles have a way of becoming challenges for people like Marge Matthews. She had already faced the problems of being a single mother, raising Bill alone from the time he was ten months of age. She had become a secretary to pay the bills, later assuming executive secretarial responsibility and learning business skills as well.

All this time, the still, small voice had been speaking. The Holy Spirit was tugging. There seemed to be a purpose for Marge's life at a new level of involvement in the church, where she was an active and faithful part of the laity. "If you are confident that God has given you gifts and graces to be used in the ministry of Christ, step out in the assurance that God's purpose will prevail," she says now to others as she once told herself. Answering the Spirit, she applied for admission to the study program for local pastors. Just three weeks later she was standing on tiptoe behind a pulpit designed for someone six feet tall. Marge Matthews was and is four feet eleven inches tall, and she maintains she is shrinking. The people were warm and receptive; even the dear lady who shook the new pastor's hand, remarking, "I always get something out of the sermon no matter who preaches it." Marjorie Matthews allows the memory of that moment to keep her humble.

She never intended to be a pioneer among clergywomen.

God's faithful seldom know where the road will lead. They only know the promise of the God who calls them forward, "I will be with you." Through days of risk, moments of doubt, and the exhilaration of the adventure, God goes with women and men who respond to the call. So it has been for Marjorie.

She spent that first summer as pastor-in-charge getting the feel of the ministry. They held a vacation church school, Bible study classes, and board and committee meetings in addition to the Sunday services. She learned not to call 7:30 P.M. meetings for farmers working in the fields until after dark. She felt the commitment of some of the church members who were at a meeting at 10 P.M. without having had their evening meal. Their commitment fed hers, that first summer. She was ready for more.

Three months later Marjorie was appointed as part-time supply pastor at Pleasant Valley, a small rural church near Alma, where she was living and working. Five years later Leaton was added to the charge and the supply pastor was a student at Central Michigan University in Mt. Pleasant, Michigan. The course of study for local pastors had fueled the fire of Marge's desire to be the best possible pastor she could be. From the beginning, nothing but the best has been her goal. She gives the best, she expects the best from others. She urges us all, lay and clergy alike, to claim the gifts that have been given to us and to use them in God's service.

What is a miracle, anyway? Is it the strange and unusual that drops one fine day from the sky? Or is it the creative use of the many opportunities that God puts before us day by day? For Marjorie it is perhaps both, but more often it is the willingness to use the opportunities, to stay on the road even when it bends and she isn't sure where it's going. She

65

was as sure then as now that her place was in the ministry. She says of that time, "The risk *was* great but I preferred the risk rather than surrender. My experience with the small churches had shown me that the people would receive a pastor who was interested in total ministry, regardless of gender. If this were true in the small, rural churches, it ought also to be true elsewhere, even though I was well aware that larger congregations tend to become increasingly conservative as their numbers grow larger." She decided that trust is the only answer. This was the same firm, unyielding trust that she was to reaffirm so many times: as a pastor, as a District Superintendent, and in that hospital bed.

"I decided to trust God for the future, and continue to prepare for the ministry in whatever ways were open to me." She said this in the midst of years of going to school and poring over the little booklet on "Steps into the Ordained Ministry." Many were the times that Marjorie faced once again the all-male Board of Ministry and wondered if the time would ever come when she would see a woman minister become a part of the interviewing and recommending process. While some of her male colleagues became staunch supporters and close friends, there were those who felt it necessary to point out the roadblocks: age, the pragmatics of college and seminary, and that the opportunities for women always would be limited (no matter how qualified).

College had been a mind-stretching experience. Marjorie felt the temptation of the academic life. Hers is the gift of the inquiring mind. College had opened new and exciting doors. Seminary would open more. Knowing deep inside that the church and the people had first claim on her time and her talent, she enrolled at Colgate Rochester Divinity School.

The timing of the Holy Spirit was perfect. The church was on the verge of recognizing that it had been impoverished by failing to call forth the ministries of so many of its daughters and sons—namely women and people from ethnic minorities. Marjorie speaks of the liberating winds that were blowing through the seminaries throughout the land. Black students were struggling, as she remembers, to move from "invisible," to "visible," to "empowerment." The women began to be a part of the same struggle. Becoming a part of this process, one that she recalls was often painful, has made of Marjorie Matthews a pastor who is more than superficially aware of the continuing struggle for the inclusion of all people at all levels of the church. Hers are more than words. She feels the pain; she participates in the battles in the name of Christ.

During the seminary years Marge also discovered the sobering truth that the parishes of western New York were not always eager to receive a female pastor. Very little had been done to prepare them for such a reception. She did, however, get some added pastoral experience in churches other than United Methodist ones.

Meanwhile, she drew upon the richness of Colgate Rochester and its variety of students, coming from many denominations and many parts of the world. Learning was far more than a classroom experience. A summer's study in Israel added to the grounding of Marjorie's theology.

Her roots sink deep into the journey of the people of God in the Old Testament. This is more than a love of scholarship. Her eyes sparkle as she gives herself to one of her first loves—teaching. She will speak of the risks taken by Abraham, the wisdom of Sarah, the meaning of the prophecy of Miriam, the calling of Moses. She is truly a women's theologian. Theology and Biblical study are for

Marjorie Matthews just as much of the heart as they are of the head. Her contribution comes from the wholeness of her life.

Returning to Michigan upon graduation, Marge was appointed to a church of two hundred members in Evart. The pastorate was a short one for two reasons. First, she had enrolled in graduate school with the intention of becoming a seminary professor. Second, the winds of the Holy Spirit got too hot to handle: lightning struck and the church burned down. Believing her talent to be more the "equipping" ministry than the building ministry, she carried out her plan to enter Florida State University, where she subsequently earned her master's degree in Religion and her doctorate in Humanities. Florida was the opportunity to delve further in biblical studies, leading her to do a specialty in Wisdom literature. Once again Marjorie developed the unique talent that enables her to unite those who learn from her with the message of God through Scripture. It comes alive, because it lives in her.

She also got what we often call the "big church" experience while in Florida. There she served as associate pastor at St. Paul's United Methodist Church, filling in for a time between the departure of one senior pastor and the arrival of another. She fondly remembers Florida friends who encouraged her to keep on "keeping on." They were confident that she would find her way through the maze of teaching, preaching, pastoring, and graduate study. And she did.

One learns that of Marjorie. She finds her way through impossibly busy schedules, keeping about her a sense of vitality. Her giving of time and talent is full measure. The bout with cancer was turned into a learning experience about time and priorities. As one who has always had a high sense of the stewardship of time and talents, she renewed her commitment after surgery to be one who gives herself only to what can be perceived as the clear call of God in her life.

The call had been abundantly clear. She once said, "It was my only hope to be able to serve the church in whatever capacity my abilities would allow. I have always been (and still am) willing to serve wherever I may be appointed. More importantly, like Paul, I am *content* to do so." Returning to Michigan once again, Marjorie was appointed to the Napoleon United Methodist Church. It had been a long road from the local pastor studies in 1961, to elder in 1965, to full membership in the West Michigan Conference in 1970. Back at Garrett in 1961, she had been one of three women in the class. The feeble jokes about women ministers flew back and forth, accompanied by feeble laughter. Marjorie had proved again and again that women in ministry are not a joke. It is the will of God working itself out in the life of the church. Her church at Napoleon discovered this as they buried, in an involvement in ministry, their early objections to their first woman pastor.

Marge's gifts as an enabler of creativity and leadership were received and appreciated. The people of Napoleon, as others in the churches she had served, were willing to take the risk, to let it happen. And it happened.

About this time an early vision became a reality. The interviewee at many sessions of the Board of Higher Education and Ministry became an interviewer. Her position there has since enabled many a female candidate to breathe just a little easier as they see among the sea of male faces the reassuring smile of a female colleague in ministry.

But new calls were being voiced. She was elected as a ministerial delegate to the General Conference of 1976.

Elected in June of 1975, she could be heard whispering to herself, "This must surely be the pinnacle!" How often we are surprised by the Holy Spirit. In November of 1975, the Holy Spirit took the form of Bishop Dwight Loder. One can almost hear him say, "Marjorie, I have for you an opportunity that you can't refuse." Since she had already said that she was content to serve wherever she might be appointed, her response was assured. More than an opportunity, more than a challenge, Marjorie Swank Matthews became the second woman District Superintendent in The United Methodist Church. (The first was Margaret Henricksen in Maine.)

It wasn't easy. It never is. Besides the expected rigor of the job itself, there was that difficulty experienced by some in recognizing the small Marjorie as an authority figure. She met the challenge with grace and with her gentle power. One must never assume that, because Marjorie Matthews is gentle and caring, she is lacking in power. Her convictions are deep and her goals are firm. She will be about the Lord's business. She says, "Proper usage of power has much to do with the demands of the Christian gospel for love and justice, and certainly should begin with the church."

The Grand Traverse District of the West Michigan Conference came to understand that the district was in capable, creative hands. Her spiritual depth added to the ministry of the district. She came as a gift, sharing the confidence needed by lay and clergy alike. The "road" became the snow-covered roads of northern Michigan.

At the time of her illness, many worried that it was all over. Marge, trusting in God for her future, whatever that might be, picked up the telephone and got back to work. The Cabinet met in her room, later at her home. When the cobalt treatments were complete, she was back on the road.

In the spring she participated in a mission tour to Puerto Rico. Her simple statement: "I believed that God must have more work ahead for me to do and would give me the strength necessary to do it. I do not know what the future may hold. I only know that God is in control of my life. I believe that I am a part of the purpose God is making known to us through the Holy Spirit. After years of silent service, we now have been given a voice. May we use that voice in God's ministry in the world."

What is the measure of one human being committed to Christ? Is it not to walk the road in faith and trust? "If you can't bear the cross, then you can't wear the crown." Marjorie Swank Matthews has carried a cross or two down that long road. All of her has risen to the task. Not asking to be a pioneer, one of our foremothers in the faith, she has nevertheless become one. The road stretches before her. There are more bends ahead. As she has placed her trust in God and continued her journey in the past, she will do so in the future. She will continue her ministry, always aware of those who draw strength and courage from her.

There are those who believe that her chance for the crown came on July 17, 1980. At the Jurisdictional Conference in Indianapolis, Marjorie Swank Matthews was elected on the twenty-ninth ballot to be the first woman bishop of The United Methodist Church. Those who know question whether or not election to that high office is in reality the crown. For Marge, now fulfilling her ministry as the episcopal leader of the Wisconsin Area, it was another open door, a bend in the road, the willingness to serve wherever appointed. Speaking with her is hearing of the new ideas, new challenges, new goals for ministry in her four years in Wisconsin. World peace, ethnic minorities; these are among her most precious concerns. She will allow God to speak through her position of leadership and influence in church and nation. She will be a part of keeping The United Methodist Church true to its heritage of commitment to peace, to the poor, and to the disenfranchised. Marjorie Matthews is as she has always been; a minister of Jesus Christ, committed to service in his church.

VII

A Beginning . . . Together

Mary Miller-Vikander

"This whole placement process sure has a nervous way of activating one's prayer life!" The twinkle in Tom's eyes revealed he knew the full irony and humor of his comment. He looked up to catch my chuckle in response.

Tom was finishing his residency in Family Practice as I graduated from seminary. We were poring over maps, preparing a list of mutually attractive locations to suggest for placement. This was our first step across the murky waters of the denomination's placement system. We felt naïve and vulnerable. Yet we recognized that we were not the only inexperienced ones. The denomination itself was entering a nervous, new phase of ministry—that of interviewing and receiving pastors who were women.

It was as recently as 1976 that the annual meeting of the Evangelical Covenant Church confirmed the Spirit's call of women into the ordained ministry. The church family, rooted in the Spirit's revival breath that blew through the Lutheran State Church of Sweden in the nineteenth century, finds its life in an experiential faith in Christ. The denomination's heart clings to the authority of Scripture as the Word of God. It affirms and cherishes the historic

confessions of the Christian church, but finds its unique-
ness in a refusal to emphasize creedal interpretations over
the Word itself. We also believe fellowship based on the
Word of God and new life in Christ can rise above personal
and theological disagreement, calling all believers to mutual
dialogue and responsible, personal freedom in God's love.

The 1976 annual meeting remained true to this heritage.
The representatives studied, argued, prayed, discussed,
and voted. After the dust had settled, the Covenant had
voted for continued growth and inclusive fellowship in
Christ.

It had made an imaginative choice. In reality, living with
it would mean drastic changes and growth—inclusion of
women in the seminary as Master of Divinity students, in
the ministerium of brothers as sisters, and in congregational
families as pastoral leaders.

My decision to enter seminary was long in coming. Ever
since coming to cognitive faith, I had felt the inner pull of the
Spirit inclining my heart toward ministry. Entering a large
state university, I announced to my academic advisor that I
wished to enter ministry upon graduation and that he
should assign me courses appropriately. I can still picture
the sarcastic amusement on his face as he replied, "We'll see
how you feel in four years."

Four years later I began working for a large para-church
youth ministry. Women staff members in the program were
expected to work only with the girls, while the men on the
staff received the more visible tasks of speaking and
teaching. This was satisfying for a while. But the
not-so-subtle sexism and disregard for my abilities of
preaching and pastoring began to dishearten me. Why
could the program not encourage diversity of gifts assigned
by the Spirit, not gender? I confess to displaying anger in my
third and fourth year in that program. I was increasingly

being cast as the scrapper for women's leadership. Discouraged and frustrated, I saw a door closing.

During this time, I became involved in the powerful ministry of a local Covenant church. The worship was moving, the intergenerational love was real, the exercise of abilities was rich in fullness, and the spiritual struggles honest. I knew the denomination was discussing women's ordination: perhaps a door was opening.

Maybe I could minister within the church's structure! But could I handle the academic load of graduate school? If only I could get out of the Greek requirement! What would this move do to my social life? My questions all seemed to focus on my inabilities and identity rather than on the theological and pragmatic issues of women's being in pastoral ministry. I decided against plunging into the difficult core courses of the Master of Divinity degree, choosing instead to wade noncommittally, as a part-time student, through two electives.

On the first Sunday of that quarter I was listening to a church announcement about the women's ordination discussion. The pastor concluded the report by saying, "This is especially significant in light of the fact that one of our own members, Mary Miller, has entered seminary this week." Astonishment left me breathless! Why does he look so proud? Sitting in the alto section of the choir, I felt, or at least imagined, dozens of eyes turning toward my blushing face. Yet something in the incident conveyed the notion that this had implications beyond my personal life. It tied my growth to that of the congregation and even the denomination. I smile to remember that embarrassed naïveté And I thank that pastor, and others, who had confidence in my ability to pastor long before I did.

The turning point in the denomination's progress occurred during my first year as a full-time seminary student. The upper two classes were made up only of men, the lower two classes of both men and women. By my senior year, all four classes were mixed.

The men and women who studied in my class were close Christian friends. North Park is one of the few theological schools that encourage their academic faculty to have previous pastoral experience. Their pastoral care and academic prodding easily included women as well as men, and provided modeling for the faith community in areas of inclusive language, images, authors, and guest lecturers. The one woman on the faculty, a Christian Education instructor, had the integrity to tell the master of Divinity students, "I am not your role model. I am a Christian educator, not a preacher and pastor." We would value that honesty as we struggled with the fact that there were no women as pastoral role models in our church who would breathe imagination into ministerial identity.

The first women who graduated and were ordained by the Covenant struggled with the pastoral role and chose to minister elsewhere. Two became hospital chaplains, one a psychotherapist. One became pastor of a church for two years and then went on to pursue further theological education.

Those desiring pastoral office would find difficulty. "Ordaining women pastors will never be a problem for the Covenant. It is placing them in churches that will be!" rang the seminary dean's realistic prophecy. No wonder Tom and I were so nervous as we cross-referenced cities in which we both could work!

Only two women presently pastor churches in our denomination. I minister in southern Michigan, and my colleague in northern Indiana. We feel the loneliness of high visibility and need each other for support. One Monday I announced to my husband, "I'm going to attend the first meeting of the Women Pastors of the Covenant today."

"Sounds impressive. What's on the agenda?" he asked.

"Eating and talking. I'm meeting Janet at the state line for lunch. I'm tired of feeling alone in this goldfish bowl."

The other two women in my class were not placed in churches. Women are especially vulnerable to the placement system because of the cluttered sexist theology, false apprehensions, and fears of change that may exist in the people in any point of the process. After months of not being called by a church, both unplaced women felt the need to make decisions of adjustment. One decided to do post-graduate studies in Europe. The other committed herself to continue to seek a church placement.

Months later I was out for coffee with two other pastors who had graduated with me. The outrage and powerlessness we all felt in our colleague's continued lack of placement was voiced by one of the men: "I can't believe this is happening to Marilyn. She is so clearly cut out for ministry. . . . To be called by God and refused exercise of that call. . . . She should be a pastor before me." I felt a blessing in his words. For in them there was the definite undertone that we, as young pastors, as men and women, as congregational leaders, as denominational members, are in this change and growth together.

We women are joining the ministerium's brothers as sisters. I bring to that fellowship the sense of loyalty, camaraderie, sibling rivalry, group humor, and common struggle that any such kinship member does. Yet the newness of the relationship requires time and negotiation before comfortable friendship develops.

I attended my first ministers' retreat as an intern pastor. The retreat was held at a conference camp which had a long building of large, crude bunk rooms in which all of the retreat's registrants could be roomed. The registration committee wondered how to house the one woman. They found a nicely furnished, separate cabin that was usually reserved for guest speakers. When they approached me with its possible use, I hedged. Do I allow myself the privileges of one who needs to be pampered, protected; who, even in quality of sleeping quarters, is different from the rest of the family? I asked them instead for one of the large empty rooms. I made the right decision, but I also paid for it. The paper-thin walls of the bunkhouse could not blot out the loud snoring of someone in the next room: I was awake all night!

Another retreat presented a different problem. It was designed for both pastors and spouses. I was walking down a long hallway toward the pastors' session when a woman I had never met, and would not recognize again, came out of a side door and asked, "Would you like to come to the wives' meeting?" Without thinking or breaking stride, I said, "No, thanks," and continued on. I have mentally replayed this incident many times. Why did she invite me? To include me? To stop me from being a pastor? Should I have sought her out afterward? I don't know.

Acceptance is a progressive attitude. I felt it during my one year internship in a local group of ministers who met weekly for theological discussion. I was early for my first meeting and sat down to wait. As the older pastors came in, they all sat on the opposite side of the discussion table. My presence was awkward for them. By the end of the year, they felt comfortable enough to ask me to present a theological and ethical discussion on the topic of abortion. I regretted having to leave their fellowship before acceptance made the further step of including me in all theological subjects, even those that are not "women's subjects."

I treasure membership in the Covenant Ministeriums,

especially the great hymn-singing sessions of the group. But I was unprepared at one session when, in the middle of the robust "All Hail the Power of Jesus' Name!" someone cried, "Women on the third verse!" I knew I was the only woman in the room. My face must have displayed panic, for the whole room sent up a roar of laughter. It had the ring of acceptance.

One of the tenderest but most frustrating tasks that women pastors have is to answer the many "curiosity questions" of our brothers. "Do you attend the men's prayer breakfast?" "What will you do if and when you have children?" "You wear a robe?" "Doesn't your husband mind all your evening meeting time?" "Tell the truth, aren't you afraid to preach?" "You mean your husband will move when you change churches?" "Aren't you nervous when it's a man that needs counsel?" Such questions even become a spontaneous part of my ordination interviews. I value the questions because they show that those who ask them trust me enough to risk their previously unspoken apprehensions about women pastors and are open to growing in friendship with me and my role. The frustration is the consistently subtle sexism that is revealed in each new friend's repetitions of the same old inquiries. It is sometimes hard to answer with genuine freshness. It may be my umpteenth time of answering the questions, but it is the inquirer's first time to dare to approach a woman who chose the pastorate.

That patient, consistent reconciliation is also needed with the congregational families in which women assume pastoral leadership. Some people have trouble affirming the integration of feminine identity and pastoral office. Those who feel they are mutually exclusive qualities argue, or vote, against a church's call of a woman pastor. Most people, however, are not fully aware of the tension they feel over the integration, and, almost unknowingly, choose to emphasize only one of the attributes. Innocent comments revealing a person's discomfort are part of a church's initial acceptance behavior. Some negate the feminine side. "Mary, you look so serious when you preach without makeup." In this person's eyes my daily makeup and curled hair were not to be seen in the pulpit. Others avoid the professional role. "Meet Mary, she works at our church." Do I add "as a minister"? There is yet a third group of comments, that which focuses on the novelty of it all. "This is our woman pastor, isn't that fun?" Ha, dear. Four years of seminary to be the life of the party!

It takes time for a pastor and congregation to get to know each other. I was speaking at a Thanksgiving luncheon for our retirement-aged women during the early months of a church pastorate. After a fabulous meal, the chairwoman stood to introduce me. "We have a special treat this meeting. Our little Mary has agreed to speak to us on a Thanksgiving theme." My reaction was mixed; I felt approval, but disappointment. Her words spoke of her deep affection and acceptance of me as a friend and a speaker. But it also denied my adult role as pastor. You can imagine the depth of my personal pleasure the next month when this chairwoman freely introduced me as "Pastor Mary."

As parishioners get to know me, they discover I am like any other pastor. I study, preach, sing hymns, offer hospital prayers, shake hands, lead meetings, make calls to the homebound, and love morning worship. I am also just like any other woman. I work on my flower garden, love to go out and eat, talk to my cat, value Saturdays with my husband, and, as the saying goes, put my pantyhose on one leg at a time. It is incredible to watch people grow into friendship with me and into the realization that I am a whole person. It is then that their initial apprehensions and anxieties dissipate.

One middle-aged man had cast the sole vote against the church's request to have me candidate. He wanted the church to contact an elderly male pastor in order to enhance visitation with the elderly. I, too, share concern for our older members and spoke of their needs freely and often. But it was not until he himself was hospitalized that he realized the genuineness of my concern, the consistency of my prayers on his behalf, as well as for all the church's members. Shortly after his recuperation we were invited to his home for dinner for a relaxed, fun evening, one of friendship and acceptance.

Sometimes that newfound trust is revealed in surprising ways. "Mary, are you busy?" I was in the crowded narthex during the post-worship coffee hour with a young woman who had voiced some strong doubts about calling a woman as a pastor. "It seems you're always busy and I never get a chance to say this. This may not be the best time but—I love you," she pronounced and gave me a hug. It took only a second to feel the full impact of that message: my eyes filled with warm tears.

Other notes of acceptance are more subtle. The ten-year-old's pencil drawing on the bulletin cover of me preaching. The confirmand's personal confession of faith that used both feminine and masculine images of God. The eighty-year-old man's "Hello, Reverend," each Sunday morning. The confidential phone calls about personal health problems. The spontaneous invitation to go out for ice cream. The teasing over the length of my last name. Even the bored glance to the wristwatch in a lengthy meeting.

But in the daily experience with ministry, it is Tom's consistent, committed companionship that is my greatest support. His self-security and aggressive love continue to encourage and enable me in this nontraditional role.

Tom also knows the mixed blessing of being a "pastor's husband," an undeveloped role in terms of congregational expectations. He has loved that freedom to use his personal gifts in service to the church, rather than being assigned expected tasks as many "pastor's wives" are. But he also knows the loneliness of being the denomination's only pastor's husband. Our present church fellowship is becoming more familiar with and solidly confident of Tom, not just as a man, a Christian, and a doctor, but as my husband. This is a big step in acceptance, for not only do the members face their own feelings about me as a woman pastor, but they also face their own acceptance of Tom in his nontraditional support of my work. We felt the congregation's strong affirmation of that relationship when it knew it wanted Tom to share in the blessing and celebration of my ordination, officially voting to give him the status of delegate to the denomination's meeting at which the ceremony occurred. Tom and I and this affirming congregation stand within the denomination as a healthy example of new growth.

I regret that I cannot write this chapter twenty years from now. Another generation of insight will have added to our denomination's growth. Presently, each woman who pastors in the Covenant is the "first" to serve—as one of a clergy couple, co-pastor, associate pastor, solo pastor, senior pastor. I pray that twenty years' growth will let such pioneers become settlers, fully included in the many facets and job descriptions of congregational and denominational leadership.

How will that next generation evaluate us? Will they think we women were too compromising? Too angry? Too naïve? Will they feel the denomination minimized the issue? Was afraid of it? Failed to give theological training to congregations and pastors? Neglected a currently undiscussed doctrine? Dragged its feet?

I hope that I shall still be pastoring when the answers to such questions begin to emerge. For I love the Covenant, my criticism of her is full of affection. She is the church who birthed, nourished, comforted, corrected, and supported me. And I am proud of her recent remarkable steps of growth to affirm the Spirit's call of both men and women as pastors. God, who moves and loves in all of earth's history, is a part of what we are doing.

VIII

Expression of a Vision

Janet Gifford-Thorne

For the first two years following graduation from Colgate Rochester Divinity School in Rochester, I served as associate minister on a three-minister staff with a church in Plainfield, New Jersey. One day the telephone rang. It was a call from the chairman of the search committee of the Plumbrook Baptist Church in Sterling Heights, Michigan. My résumé interested them. Would I be willing to be considered for the position of pastor? That telephone call was the beginning of a relationship with a congregation that has been very productive and rewarding.

Since my arrival in March, 1975, we have traveled several roads together: from decay to growth, from hopelessness to vision, from depression to optimism, from a marginal operation to a many-faceted center of Christian ministry. Today, Plumbrook Baptist Church is characterized by its vitality. The congregation and I are engaged in a thriving ministry. Over ninety percent of the resident membership attends worship regularly. The congregation lives out a healthy balance of the two important criteria for Christ's body: a gathered community in worship, study, and nurture; a scattered community in ministry.

84

Why did Plumbrook Baptist Church call me when most American Baptist Churches, like most other Protestant churches, would not consider a woman for the position of pastor? Why did they decide to interview me when most churches would not even take the time to study the résumé of a minister who happens to be a woman?

They were an open group of people. They were willing to consider new ideas and to venture out beyond the experience of the past. The committee had determined at the outset of their year-long search for a pastor that they would consider candidates on the basis of quality of personhood and skill in ministry, rather than on the basis of sex, race, or any other distinctions. They said that they were looking for someone who would perform the responsibilities of the position with ability and determination.

They were receptive to the suggestion of their Area Minister (whose job included assisting the American Baptist Churches in metropolitan Detroit in their quests for pastoral leadership), that they study my résumé as a candidate with real potential for the job.

The Search Committee (Pulpit Committee) is the central factor in ministerial placement in American Baptist Churches. The principle of local church autonomy means that each congregation selects its own pastor. By congregational vote a representative committee is formed to act on behalf of the whole body. They are vested with the power to seek résumés from the denominational placement service, from seminaries, from the area minister, and to interview qualified candidates.

The decision is in their hands. When they have come to a consensus on a candidate, after a process of several months to a year or more, they recommend that individual to the congregation. The congregation hears that person who comes "to candidate" as a guest preacher and to meet the congregation. A vote is taken. In most cases the congregation votes overwhelmingly to accept the choice of the committee.

Of twenty-five persons considered seriously for the position at Plumbrook, twenty-four were men, one was a woman. The committee did not think that their policy statement of openness to all résumés would actually lead them to call a woman. But my credentials matched what they were looking for in leadership.

Through the interview process we discovered that our ideas about the nature and purpose of the Christian Church were complementary. We sensed that we would work well together. They decided I was the person they were seeking. I decided to venture out in my ministry and become their pastor. When one member of the Pulpit Committee went home and told his wife that the committee had made its selection and was going to recommend that the church call a twenty-six-year-old woman minister from New Jersey, she uttered a shocked, "You've done what?!!"

Myths and images of what some unknown experience might bring melt away in the real-life encounter. Right from the beginning, relationships started to build between me and the people of the congregation. The pastoral ministry offered was more important than the package the pastor came in.

Plumbrook Church was at a low point in its history when I began. It had been organized twelve years previously, in 1963, as a new church in the suburban area north of Detroit. Even in the best of circumstances, the founding years of a new congregation require hard work and determination. The Plumbrook congregation had persevered when many other new churches had folded, but it was barely surviving.

The highly mobile population in the surrounding area had an impact on church involvement. Looking at the membership was like standing in one place and watching a passing parade. Without persistent efforts in church growth the congregation had dwindled severely as it entered its second decade of life. Worship attendance ranged from thirty to forty. There were only fifty-six active resident members. To many it appeared Plumbrook Church was dying.

Churches located in areas like Plumbrook, where there is a highly mobile population, face a great challenge in their growth. They must develop ways of inviting new people into their midst continually. If they do not concentrate energy and imagination on this ministry of outreach and receptivity toward others, simple attrition will result in a diminishing congregation, unable to carry on a vigorous ministry.

I sensed the qualities of grit and determination in the people. They were survivors. The question that hovered over the people's minds and surfaced often in conversation during the early days of my pastorate was this: "Will we be able to keep the doors of the church open?" The unanswered question I faced as a newly installed pastor was this: "Will we be able to change from a 'survivor's' church where survival is the consuming goal to a 'ministry' church where we live out a vital Christian ministry?"

I worked to instill a sense of purpose and direction among the members. I was convinced that when people have a vision of who they are, of what they represent, of where they are heading, then they will achieve more than they ever dreamed possible. That conviction has been borne out in my experience at Plumbrook.

I hold a particular vision that motivates my ministry. My understanding is that all Christians are called by Christ into ministry. The ministries differ according to the gifts we possess. My ministry is to help others discover their gifts and their particular callings.

The meaning of the term *laity* comes from the Greek *laos,* which translates as "the whole people of God." This informs my understanding that the ministry of Christ belongs to the whole people. I see my responsibility as pastor to empower others for ministry.

The location of ministry has no restrictive boundaries. Ministry, i.e., acting on behalf of Christ, happens wherever we are, in the church and in the world. For purposes of clarity I speak of the ministry of the gathered church and the ministry of the scattered church. The church gathers for worship, study, and nurture, then scatters so that its members will incarnate the presence of Christ in their jobs, at home, at school, and in community pursuits.

From the beginning of my pastorate, I made it clear that the people of Plumbrook Church were ministers and that the destiny of the congregation belonged to us all. This sense of ownership which the congregation holds about their church has been one of the prime factors in moving out of a period of decay and hopelessness into a time of growth and vision.

I perceive the ministry of empowerment to be one of releasing people for responsible action. A mental image I carry with me that illustrates this point is one of a juggler juggling a set of oranges. The task of the pastor is not to juggle oranges as an enjoyable demonstration for others to watch, but rather to hand the oranges, i.e., the ministry, on to people for them to handle.

Through my experience as the pastor at Plumbrook, the congregation and I and the wider church are gaining important knowledge about the role of women in the pastoral ministry. A positive contribution that women are making to the whole church has to do with a new style of leadership. Growing within me is the conviction that women clergy are often gifted for a style of sharing in mutual ministry with the laity. We are not perceived in as authoritarian a light as male clergy are. We do not have to overcome generations of expectation that the pastor is a go-it-alone juggler, or a dominating figure. The women's liberation movement has reminded us to celebrate the collaborative style of shared leadership. A man who is a member of Plumbrook Church observed, "The reason the church does what it does the way it does it, is partially because of a talent of Jan's for getting people to do this and partially because she is a woman. The fact that she is a woman, people don't look at her as much as an authority figure, so they feel freer to do things and less like she's dominating."

I have met with some resistance in my empowering the ministry of others. Often, after reaching some new stage of responsible ministry, a woman or man will look back and reveal, "When I brought that problem to you and you wouldn't let me drop it in your lap or take it away from me, I was so angry. When you suggested that I had the resources to solve that dilemma or try that new venture in life, I was so frightened." But in almost every instance the people do venture forth and grow exceedingly in ability and self-concept as Christ's ministers.

I heard a member of Plumbrook Church describe my style of ministry by saying, "Jan's style of pastoring is that she holds you with one arm while pushing you to self-confident independent ministry with the other. Her habit of repressing her own insights and asking, 'What do we do now?' causes others to take charge." I really love the thousands of opportunities the pastoral ministry affords for sparking creativity in people. Creative people become active people.

A leave of absence is an opportunity for the pastor to step back and let those active people take charge. There are so many situations in which a leave of absence may occur that the learning coming out of our direct experience at Plumbrook has universal application to diverse settings. A planned leave of absence may be undertaken for obtaining specialized training, as a time for research and writing, for surgical purposes, or for vacation.

One question that intrigues the mind when consideration is given having a woman as pastor is, "What would be the experience for congregation and pastor if she were to become pregnant?" My story includes this experience of pregnancy and subsequent planned leave of absence.

The news of my pregnancy was received with delight by the congregation. We agreed that I would be away from the job for six weeks following the birth of my baby. The leave of absence was a combination of three weeks paid maternity leave, followed by three weeks of my regular vacation time.

Over a period of five months, the leaders of the congregation and I planned for the leave. Our goal was that, during my absence, the ministry of the gathered church would not skip a beat in being carried out completely by the laity. We accomplished our goal.

We concentrated our energies on preparing people to lead the church in three major areas of the pastoral role: worship, pastoral care, and administration. Thirty people secured training or were otherwise prepared to minister in these areas. Sermons were written, worship celebrations planned, training in hospital and prospective-new-member calling accomplished, administrative duties to be delegated were outlined. As the due date drew near, the congregation commissioned the thirty for their particular ministries within the church at a worship celebration. We were ready.

My daughter Elizabeth was born in the early hours of

Friday, May 26, 1978. Her birth signaled the beginning of two very important new identities; mine as a mother, and the congregation's as a people equipped to do the ministry within the church.

Without exception, the laity described the maternity leave as a thoroughly positive experience for Plumbrook Baptist Church. My planned leave was a very significant chapter in the life of the church. For a short, intensive time period, a large number of laity concentrated their ministry within the structure of the church. When I returned to work, they were released from this focus of ministry. We could then return to the ongoing rhythm of shared ministry.

Today my energies are devoted primarily to ministry within the church. A group of gifted and capable laity share in this arena with me. For many of the laity, their primary ministries are found in the places of their vocations, including job and home.

The reason we have energy for both church and world ministry in a congregation that numbers around 120 members is that we keep the operation of the church "clean and lean." The structure of the church is simple.

In my opinion, one of the greatest wastes of human energy on behalf of the Church is the way in which so many congregations are structured to gobble up the laity's time and energy in meaningless activity instead of purposeful action. I have learned that organizational structure can serve to either block or empower the ministries of people.

An important part of my ministry is the mobilization of precious and limited human resources. At Plumbrook we designed a new organizational structure. A single Council of nine people serves as the center of the design. It, along with two standing committees, is the only fixed part of our structure. The rest is totally flexible. The result of our having reshaped the structure allows us to mobilize people around particular needs. When a certain number of people are needed to handle a given task, they join forces. When the task is accomplished, they are free to rest or go on to another ministry task. People are able to choose the areas of the church's life that interest them.

We have come a long way, the congregation and I, since I began my pastorate. Decay has given way to growth. Hopelessness has been transformed into vision. Depression has been converted into optimism. Plumbrook Baptist Church is now a many-faceted center of Christian ministry.

You have seen this story unfold through my eyes. Another perspective is offered by the moderator of the church, speaking to a metropolitan-wide training workshop for church leaders. "Plumbrook is not a building in Sterling Heights; it is not just a group of Christians gathered for worship on Sunday morning; it is a collection of God's ministers, priests and prophets, striving to be Christ's body in the arenas of their daily lives. . . . It is difficult to share with you our model. We have just begun to discover its shape and meaning. God has much more to reveal to us as we continue with the discovery of our ministries. I *can* share with you our enthusiasm of new discovery, the excitement of experiencing God's love, the insecurity of newness, the challenge of stretching to reach the stature of Christ, and the peace that comes with fulfillment."

In the calm of the evening, when I am bicycling or reading a good book, my mind stretches out over the expanse of my life. As with others in the congregation; ministry, family, and self are distinct spheres and yet blended parts of who I am.

I offer my story to you in the hope that my quest for meaning and purpose might resonate with your own experience. If you have identified resistance within yourself to women in the pastoral ministry, I hope that you will shed your opposition and direct your energy into working for more opportunity for women to minister as pastors.

We are living through times of a great awakening; within women to their God-given talents, and within the church to the ministry of women. On the whole, women are further along in the discovery of their talents than the church is in allowing the exercise of those talents. I feel fortunate that my gifts were not atrophied, like those of some women who are forced to spend lengthy apprenticeships.

I feel the delight of my ministry's having found expression. I close with deep appreciation to the people of Plumbrook Baptist Church.

IX

Men Can Be Pastors, Too

Barbara Jurgensen

When the Bishop of the Illinois District of the American Lutheran Church asked me to serve as the interim pastor of First Lutheran Church of Logan Square in Chicago in the fall of 1978, he told me that so many members of this once very large (1200-member) congregation had moved to the suburbs that it looked as if it would have to close; certainly within three years, perhaps in two, or even one. It appeared that some of the remaining 179 people were just hoping to keep it open long enough to celebrate Christmas together one last time.

He assured me that it needed a pastor, that I should go in and minister to those who were left, and that there would be no mark against me when it did finally have to close its doors.

Arriving at the handsome old brown brick church that fall, I asked how many seventh- and eighth-graders they had for confirmation class. When they said four, I said, "That's not enough to really have a good time together. Look around among your neighbors and friends and bring me the names of as many unchurched young people as you can."

By the time class started we had rounded up six unchurched young people to add to our own four for a total of ten. When we confirmed the seven eighth-graders the following May, it was the largest class in many years.

One of the young people they brought in, Randy, had never been to Sunday school or church, and faith became very meaningful to him. One Saturday morning we made a banner in confirmation class, then went to the chancel to hang it up. When Randy finally got it in place, he sat down in the pastor's chair behind the pulpit, partly to rest and admire his work and partly, I think, to see what it would feel like to be seated there. Watching him run his hand over the scrollwork of one of the arms, I said, "Randy, maybe someday you'll be sitting in a chair like that."

As I drove home later that day and got to thinking that Randy has never known any pastor but me, I wondered if I should have said, "You know, Randy, men can be pastors too."

The Beginning of a Long Journey

I have never thought of myself as being particularly restricted by being a woman. In Excelsior, the suburb of Minneapolis where I grew up, women did all sorts of intriguing things—the woman next door had held various positions of leadership in a national organization, another served on the Board of Regents of the University of Minnesota, a third was a well-known sculptor, and three were nationally published authors. In our family, women had been teachers for generations.

I fully expected to do something exciting with my life, just as these women had done. I wanted to marry and have children, but I also expected to play some creative part in the

95

world around me. Whenever my sister, two cousins, and I would play house, one of them would be the father, one the mother, one the child, and I would be the writer. While they stirred up mud pies, I was busy writing stories and light verse.

My earliest memories of the church are of joining in the responsive reading of the Psalms on Sunday morning and being amazed at the things I found there; that God, the Creator of all, cares tenderly for each of us, and that he is seeking to make us his people.

I married at twenty, finished my last year in college, and since then have been a pastor's wife and the mother of three children who are now grown. Two are now married, and I am delighted to be a grandmother. I have also been a candidate for the North Dakota House of Representatives, a Girl Scout leader, a delegate to the famous (or infamous) 1968 Democratic National Convention in Chicago, a PTA president, a high school teacher and librarian, a writer-editor for a national corporation, a lover of the out-of-doors, and an officer in various civic organizations. And always a writer. Over the years I have had fourteen books published on a variety of topics: ecology, ministry, the Old Testament prophets, religious satire, living in a day of limited resources, problems of teenagers, plus several individual and collective biographies.*

I was reared in the Congregational Church, and since I did not know at the time that women could serve as ministers in that denomination, I decided that I would

*The titles include *Leaping Upon the Mountains; All the Bandits of China; Oh, Please . . . Not Bethlehem; Men Who Dared; Parents, Ugh; Quit Bugging Me; The Lord Is My Shepherd, But; You're Out of Date, God? Don't Bug Me, Preacher; Some Day We've Got to Get Organized; God Probably Doesn't Know I Exist; How to Live Better on Less; A Polluter's Garden of Verses; The Prophets Speak Again.*

attend a school such as Union Seminary and teach theology and Bible in one of our denomination's schools in India. Then I met Dick, became a Lutheran pastor's wife, and have done my ministry as a lay person in his congregations in a variety of ways—Bible study leader, choir director, Sunday school teacher—and have also written articles and curriculum materials for a number of denominations.

When we moved to Chicago in 1973, I finally was able, because we lived in the neighborhood of the Southside cluster of seminaries, to get the theological education I had been seeking. I began studying at the Lutheran School of Theology, and transferred to the Divinity School of the University of Chicago from which I received a Master of Divinity degree. I am completing my work on a doctorate in Old Testament. I also was granted the Master of Divinity degree by Lutheran Seminary in St. Paul after fulfilling their requirements through my studies in Chicago.

When the Bishop asked me to go to First Lutheran Church, I knew I was replacing a man who had resigned after only eleven months to return to school. The members were not ready to think about calling a new pastor—they had some grief to work through, and I tried to help them with that. Several months later, the time came for them to start thinking about finding a new pastor. I was here, they knew me well, and I think they had recognized that I had not come as a crusader for the women's movement, but as a person doing ministry. Rather than arguing about women's rights, I have hoped that by doing the work I would demonstrate that a woman can do it, thus making further argument unnecessary. I have been very fortunate in being placed in a congregation that is both committed and flexible.

One of our main emphases has been on building up the

97

Sunday school. The first fall we had eighteen enrolled from age three through grade eight, an average of less than two per grade, a discouraging situation for teachers and students. Then, during that year, a family broke up and four of the eighteen moved away. But we've been trying some new things to build attendance, knowing that the future of our congregation depends on bringing in younger members. The first Sunday of each month we have a free pancake breakfast before Sunday school to attract new children. Rather than wait until the end of the year to give attendance pins, we've been giving lapel pins with Christian symbols—a dove, a fish—for each of ten Sundays. We've also been encouraging the children to bring unchurched friends by letting those who do so select a foreign coin from an ornate metal box.

By my third year the Sunday school attendance was up to twenty-five, but it has been slow going in a neighborhood that once was Norwegian Lutheran, but today is at least one-half Spanish Catholic.

When we were preparing to hold Vacation Church School with a neighboring church during my second summer, the teachers were lamenting that they usually had only about twenty children.

"Well, let's go out and bring some more in," I suggested. We had a parade around the block for about fifteen minutes the first morning and also went out with registration blanks in the afternoon. The first day we had twenty-two children, the second fifty-two. The teacher said, "Enough! We aren't prepared to handle any more than this."

We were hoping that some of these new students, mostly Hispanic, would register for Sunday school in the fall. They did visit a few times, but did not return with any regularity. Now I have learned that some of them were embarrassed about their Spanish accent when they were asked to read in class. We have discussed the problem at our teachers' meeting and from now on our teachers will ask for volunteers to do necessary reading. We have invited the children back and are expecting they will come, and we have three Hispanic girls in the Carol Choir.

It probably will be some time, however, before the Spanish adults and our members will mix comfortably. Our neighborhood has the highest incidence of gang-related crime in the city of Chicago, probably due largely to the Anglo male teenagers' trying to keep the Hispanic male teenagers off their turf. I have witnessed three rumbles directly below my second-floor office window, the contenders bearing rocks and bricks one time, rocks and car aerials another time, and beer bottles the third, with garbage can lids for shields. Fortunately no one was hurt; it was mostly a lot of yelling, threats, and running at each other.

All available space on the sides of neighborhood buildings seems to be spray-painted with the names of the gangs: FREAKS, DEMONS, PSYCHOS. Garage doors suffer the same fate. As a result, some of our members are unfortunately, but understandably, a bit reluctant to invite adult Hispanics; some have expressed a fear that the newcomers will take over the church "the same way they have taken over the neighborhood." Our people tend to overlook the fact that generally it is the reaction of the Anglos rather than the actions of the Hispanics that is the cause of many of the problems.

I have seen many good things during these years at First Lutheran. During my first year we baptized more than twenty people, many of them young people and adults. Our youth work is reviving with camp and other activities, and our membership has gone up to over two hundred in spite of the numerous deaths of an aging congregation. Month after month our church attendance has been the highest in five years. Those who were watching to see what would happen in this, the first ALC congregation in the Illinois District to be pastored solely by a woman, must see by now that it can work. I give my deepest thanks to my congregation who have made it possible, to my male colleagues, and to my District, who could not have been more accepting. And to my husband, who wants to see the church be what it should be.

Why Did It Take So Long?

I can remember so well the "Men for the Ministry" conferences that our denomination used to have—and perhaps still does in some places. Each pastor was asked to look through his congregation for young men in high school or college who might have the potential of becoming good pastors. He was then to invite them to a weekend on the nearest church college or seminary campus where they would be told of the need for more pastors, given a glimpse of the greatness of the calling, and asked to search their hearts to see if God possibly might be calling them to serve him in such a way.

Meanwhile, those of us who were young women were saying, "We feel called to serve our Lord in the ministry. Here we are; send us." But the answer we received was, "You can be directors of religious education or Sunday school teachers. Now, don't any of you young men feel that perhaps the Lord is placing his hand on your shoulder and saying, 'Come, I want you to serve me'?"

It isn't, I believe, that the Lord hasn't been calling women into the ministry, but rather that the church hasn't been listening. Or, if it is only in recent days that He has been calling women, perhaps these are the latter days spoken of by the prophet Joel, days in which our sons and our daughters shall prophesy, "prophesying" meaning basically "speaking for someone else." Proclaiming God's freeing Word certainly is the type of prophesying needed by the church in our day, and I believe that women, as mature Christians, should play a very responsible role in this work.

In many of our seminaries today women comprise thirty to forty percent of the entering class. What will these women find when they finish their studies? Are church members who have become accustomed to women high school teachers, women college professors, and women doctors, dentists, and lawyers going to be slow at letting women into a profession in which they can serve equally well? Is there anything in preaching and leading worship, in teaching and directing an educational program, in managing the church "household" and in giving pastoral care that women can't do? And dare the church any longer keep women from taking a full place in the life of the church?

I am also concerned about the fact that many seminaries still have no more than a token woman on the staff, perhaps only an instructor in Christian Education who is not looked on as part of the academic faculty. Certainly there are beginning to be women trained who could fill seminary teaching positions very well and, by bringing a slightly different viewpoint, make seminary a more rounded experience for both the men and women students. This fall of 1980 I have begun teaching part time at Bethany Seminary, Oak Brook, Illinois, in addition to my parish

101

duties. Bethany has eight women on its faculty. I hope more seminaries will follow their example.

If a woman really is serious about wanting to do ministry and is not in it to prove a point, I believe bishops and call committees will sense this. We who are women may for some time yet have to be willing to serve in the smallest congregations, in the ones that are least likely, for various reasons, to get a pastor, but if we really are serious about serving, should this make any difference to us? Jesus did not demand Rome or Alexandria, he was willing to go to Bethelehem.

As women we need to develop the habit of what Luther referred to as "putting the best construction on what the other person does." I have seen a few women pastors who are almost paranoid; they can turn even the most normal conversation into an attack aimed directly at them. Again, if we are really concerned about doing ministry, we will not have time for imagining insults—or for letting them bother us if they do come.

All of us who are seriously trying to follow our Lord, whether we are ordained or not, have a ministry. Jesus never said it would be particularly easy—in fact, I remember his saying several things to the contrary. But he also promised to be with his followers.

Friends have suggested that, had I been a man with my background, the bishop probably would not have placed me in this congregation. I think that may be true. I am glad he did, but I also think that it may be some time before congregations are ready to receive women pastors in the way that they should. And so we who are women have a choice: to complain loudly (which perhaps some are called to do) or to rejoice that the opportunity to be an ordained pastor is now open to us and to receive each opportunity and each new day as a gift. I am thoroughly enjoying being a pastor.

My congregation, to which people flocked in its heyday, is now learning to reach out in a way that it never had to before. There is a real sense of satisfaction in our working together to accomplish our goal. At First Lutheran we have too much to do to worry about the gender of our pastor. We are called to be God's people in our own place, and that we are trying to do.

X

On Being First

Carolyn J. Jones

It was October 2, 1977—World Communion Sunday, and my first public appearance as Assistant Pastor of the Glenshaw Presbyterian Church. As the congregation stood to sing "Love Divine, All Loves Excelling," the words stuck in my throat and my eyes filled with tears. Looking out at rows of faces that were soon to be associated with names and personalities, I was overwhelmed by the promise and the responsibility converging in this moment. A dream was fulfilled; a new reality was just beginning. "Enter every trembling heart," we sang, and the words became my prayer.

The dream had begun to take shape only three years earlier in suburban Syracuse, New York. After working several years as Assistant Dean of Women at Syracuse University, I had discovered a new identity emerging as I began serving as half-time Associate in Christian Education at Pebble Hill Presbyterian Church, while continuing to work in the Student Affairs Office at the University. In time, friends in both situations began to affirm my gifts for ministry, gently prodding me to consider attending seminary. I was not easily moved. Finally, I realized this was the one "calling" in which I could share my faith through so many activities I thoroughly enjoy. Music, teaching, counseling, drama, public speaking, administration, program development—all are included in the work of ministry. So, I stopped resisting and went to seminary.

Now, here I was, on the threshold of a third career, discovering truth in the cliché that a new life can begin at forty!

The Glenshaw Presbyterian Church that was to nurture this new life was far more traditional than the other two I had served. In recent years I had become accustomed to modern church buildings and congregations with a fairly contemporary style of worship and service. I was "spoiled" and I knew it—and I liked it! But I had responded to the invitation to serve this congregation because I saw in it a unique opportunity for continued growth through real breadth in ministry.

I would be able to build on my experience as a teacher, although my responsibilities were not to be limited to Christian Education. My years in administration would be an asset, because they had taught me to view the programs and problems of institutions holistically. First-hand exposure to the mission of the church through three years of service as a "short-term missionary" at the American College for Girls (now Ramses College) in Cairo, Egypt, would help me to interpret the world mission of the church with both confidence and commitment. When I was presented to the Session (governing body) of this congregation shortly after my graduation from seminary, one elder asked whether or not I felt I would be able to understand people who faced the challenges of life in the "real world." How good it was to know—and to be able to say—that I had *lived* in that world for a good many years! Indeed, experience in the "real world" had been part of my preparation for ministry.

Seeing women in positions of leadership was not foreign to the Glenshaw Presbyterian Church, since they had been electing women to serve as elders since 1953, being the sixth church in Pittsburgh Presbytery to take that step. Still, I was the first woman to serve the church as a pastor, and that's different!

How often I've been reminded of the question asked by young Peter, then an astute junior high student, as I left Syracuse for seminary. "Will you be the first?" he wanted to know.

"No, Peter," I had to tell him. "There are already well over one hundred women serving as ministers in the United Presbyterian Church." Immediately I realized that, even if true, this was the wrong answer to give to someone of Peter's adventurous spirit.

"Then why bother doing it if you're not going to be first?" he wondered. Someday I must tell Peter that I was wrong, for I *was* the first clergywoman most of the people in this congregation had seen or met. In fact, I suspect that for the next decade or so, the majority of newly ordained clergywomen will discover the joys and responsibilities of being the "first" wherever they are called to serve.

Just because they are first, many women ministers may not experience the "honeymoon" period most of their male colleagues enjoy. Certainly I was aware from the outset that the Session had not voted unanimously to invite me to come to Glenshaw. In fact, one elder had walked out of the meeting at which I was presented. But I knew that I had the support of the pastor, Dr. Gordon E. Boak, since he had intentionally sought a woman assistant. We were entering this new venture together—with our eyes open.

The optimist always notes signs of hope in the midst of

challenge, and gathers strength from them. I felt it was good that no one had raised a disapproving eyebrow when I mentioned that I drove a red-and-white Monte Carlo. Nor did they flinch when I described my liturgical attire—a unique, appliquéd white robe designed to communicate both joy and dignity (made for me by friends at the Newlonsburg United Presbyterian Church where I had served as Director of Christian Education throughout my years in seminary). So it was in a spirit of hope that I began my ministry at the Glenshaw Presbyterian Church.

From the beginning I was determined not to seek acceptance as a woman pastor by appearing and acting just like a man. Unfortunately, I had no role models. In fact, until I entered seminary I had never even heard a woman preach. So I was left to forge my own answer to the question, "What does it mean to be a woman in ministry?" At the same time, a part of me was not sure that the question was even appropriate, since generalizations about clergy-*women* should be no more valid than those concerning their male counterparts. It seemed, therefore, more productive to ask, "How can I as a Christian—given my strengths and weaknesses, my age, interests, training, and background of experience—be an authentic pastor?"

Still, I had to acknowledge the fact that I *am* a woman, and that my very presence assisting in worship each week shouted "change" in the heart of an institution where some people inevitably resist changes of any sort. Thus it was important for me to move slowly during those initial months of testing and proving, allowing time for people to come to know (and trust) me before I became the visible source of other innovations.

After I had been at Glenshaw nearly two years, I risked changing the cover of the weekly bulletin one summer Sunday morning. We reproduced a sequence of drawings of the face of Jesus, rather than the standard picture of the church building, to accent the theme of the day, the Transfiguration. Even more daring, the program was folded in thirds rather than in half, as usual. One family, I am told, was absolutely horrified! Others were delighted! To paraphrase Abraham Lincoln: "You can't please all of the people all the time." But women ministers can, perhaps, guide the congregations they serve in distinguishing between change for its own sake and change that opens the way to new insights, opportunities, experiences, and forms of service.

Although I am convinced that God calls both women and men to service in the Church of Jesus Christ, I would not characterize myself as a "banner waver" for the cause. I have chosen, rather, to be an advocate for the feasibility of women's serving as pastors by carrying out the work of ministry, as I encounter it, as competently as possible. With this decision comes a responsibility.

A female legislator has observed: "Men assume office with a presumption of competence. Women assume office with the burden of proof." I have also heard a woman physician acknowledge that she has to do "more than," so as not to be accused of doing "less than," her colleagues. For now, clergywomen, too, have to be "a little bit better" in order to be considered equal to the men who have occupied the office for centuries.

For me, responding to this challenge has meant careful preparation for each occasion of pastoral leadership, whether I am preaching, teaching, or conducting a meeting. It has meant putting in a full week's work in the parish—much of it unseen and some of it at crazy hours—so that I can do my part in the work of the presbytery and synod, where female presence is sought. It has meant attending Saturday workshops and seminars in an effort to "catch up" with my age peers who have been in ministry for fifteen years. It has meant, in these first few years, too little personal time.

Learning to live with the tension of time was only part of the initial adjustment to life in ministry. I also had to learn to recognize and cope with the (often unconscious) assumptions of others. Some assumed that, because I am a woman, I would function essentially as a Director of Christian Education. Others assumed that I would take on the responsibilities of former associates, one of whom had emphasized youth ministry, and the other, visitation with the aging and homebound in the church and the community. My gender caused the church secretaries to cope with conflicting assumptions. Was I due in every morning at 9 A.M.—with "the girls"? Or, as a pastor, was I to be granted some discretion concerning my times of arrival and departure? It appeared that the presence of a "lady preacher" sharpened the varied expectations members of congregations always have of their ministers. We probably could have been more precise in interpreting my intended areas of responsibility to the congregation, but there is no assurance that that would have helped! My task was to sort out which dynamics were reactions to my being a woman, and which were the inevitable result of my assuming a staff position. I was determined not to become paranoid in the process.

Only after I had been in Glenshaw long enough to have earned the confidence of members of the congregation did I discover other expectations and concerns people had held. It was clear from the tone of their comments that some were quite surprised to discover that I could, indeed, preach an acceptable sermon. And more than one woman confessed to me that she had anticipated having a problem with the voice of a woman minister, but that I was really very easy to listen to. The daughter of a drama major, I had won Bible reading contests in my youth, and had even taught speech and coached debate teams for a few years—but I had never dreamed that my vocal apparatus would be an asset in ministry. I am now grateful in a new way for the influence of my heritage in training the God-given gift of speech.

In addition, I sensed that some people viewed my presence in worship and in meetings as a novelty to be looked at with curiosity and treated with tolerance, but not to be taken seriously. However, by May of 1979 when I was installed as Associate Pastor, it was clear that I was here to stay, at least for a while, and we began another stage in our life together as pastor and people.

My leadership style, I know, has taken some people by surprise. There is a lot of "do it yourself-er" in me. I recognize that. I have, therefore, intentionally sought to develop the approach set forth in Ephesians 4, "the equipment of the saints for the work of ministry." It is a style that renders one vulnerable to misunderstandings from without and frustration within, especially in a large congregation where many people often want their pastors to tell them what to do and think. And it would be much easier and less time-consuming for us to do just that. At the same time, I discovered that there were others, thoroughly socialized by our culture, who expected a woman minister to be a fairly passive figure. Perhaps these folk were the most surprised!

My approach has been to encourage people to ask new kinds of questions by asking questions myself, offering resources, and holding up alternative "visions" for their consideration. "What do you suppose would happen if, instead of practically eliminating all our programs in the summertime, we were to add something new one night a week?" "Given this understanding of the role of Deacons, are there other projects you'd like to consider as ways of serving our church and community?" "Help me to understand the purpose of your group a little better, and then I'll try to make some program suggestions." Sharing in the joy people experience when they discover their own ideas taking shape and coming alive through this kind of reflection encourages me to keep working at resisting the temptation to be too directive.

In reviewing these early years of ministry I discover, however, that my greatest joys have not been the result of any effort of my own. The most treasured have come in those serendipitous moments when people, in their own ways, have offered me their unique gifts of acceptance and affirmation. Shortly after I arrived in Glenshaw, a couple of the older gentlemen in the congregation, both elders, began to make a habit of stopping by my study briefly—just to chat—on their way to or from meetings of a retired men's group. The one who is still living continues to check in regularly, indicating a willingness to listen to help by his casual, "Is there anything I ought to know?"

A couple of other elders tried in their own way to help me relax the first few times I assisted in celebrating the sacrament of the Lord's Supper. After serving the congregation, they made designs of the bread remaining on the plates before returning them to me at the communion table—one lone cube of bread, a smiling face, a mini-mountain. The first time I served Communion to shut-ins, a long-time member volunteered to accompany me, to help me find the way and make the introductions. A gracious and welcome gesture!

Gradually, as people began to seek me out for personal counsel and advice on committee projects, I recognized that I was being tested, as students test a substitute teacher, to see if I were really equal to the challenge. I've had to do a fair

111

amount of homework to begin to become as familiar with annual budgets and the problems of building maintenance as I have long been with youth resources and folk hymns, but it has been time well spent. How grateful I am for one trustee who, without patronizing, talks with me about building construction, boiler operations, falling plaster, and financial matters as if he assumes I understand. The result? I do!

Affirming in a delightfully different way was the comment someone made one evening while passing my study door and hearing the clickety-clack of the typewriter. "You should *never* let anybody know you can type like that," the voice warned. As these people have been willing to venture beyond the security of stereotypes, they have freed me to grow in ministering to them—to move from "proving myself" as a clergywoman, to loving them as their pastor. It is rare now for a member of the congregation to introduce me to an acquaintance as the resident curiosity— "I'd like you to meet our lady minister." Now it is, matter-of-factly, "This is our associate pastor" (leaving people to make their own gender distinctions).

At the same time, I am convinced that some of the expressions of appreciation I receive for my prayers, my language, my use of silence in worship, and for the way I hold infants in my arms to baptize them are directly related to the fact that I am, without question, a *woman* in ministry. The images I use in creating sermons, for example, are probably different from those a man would choose. After using the butterfly as a symbol of change and new life, I was amazed to receive as Christmas gifts, four months later, butterflies on magnets, note paper, jewelry, and a hand-painted plaque.

Admittedly, entering the parish ministry at mid-life has required patience, careful preparation, long hours, a positive outlook, and a sense of humor. But the rewards are such that I'd do it again! When I arrive at a hospital emergency room and hear a wife and daughter sigh with relief, "We were afraid they wouldn't be able to find you!" or when a patient, barely able to speak, looks up from his bed in a critical care unit and says, "I'm so glad you came," I feel blessed to be a pastor. One Sunday morning a young man, with his beautiful family in tow, lingered at the door for a moment on his way out of church and said, "I want to say what I was thinking all during church as I looked at you up there—I love you." With fringe benefits such as that, I'm persuaded that it's not bad at all—being first!

XI

Over, Around, Under, and Through

Jane Krauss Jackson

Some members of the congregation and other friends wondered why I decided to be ordained Sunday afternoon, November 24, 1974. "Why that particular day?" they asked. "Why not early in October, soon after you were called to the church? Why not in December, when there's a festive mood everywhere?"

The reasons I was immediately conscious of were those of convenience. November 24 gave the congregation and me some time to get to know one another before we celebrated together. It narrowly missed Thanksgiving preparations and avoided the Christmas rush entirely. Members of the presbytery and the seminary faculty whom I wanted to be on the ordination commission could attend then. My children, who were still members of the church I had belonged to while in seminary, could be present. My mother would drive up for the service and stay through Thanksgiving. Seminary classmates and other friends who were ordained and involved with their own church responsibilities would be free.

The religious significance of that particular Sunday was even more important than its convenience. I have felt it a continuous blessing to have been ordained and installed as pastor of Portland Avenue Presbyterian Church on Sunday, November 24, 1980, Thanksgiving Sunday, the last Sunday in the season of Pentecost.

Certainly, being ordained was something to be thankful for! Ordination had not even been a dream for me in the fall of 1970 when I enrolled in seminary to audit a course in community ministry. My youngest child, Bob, then known by his middle name, Doyle, was six and was entering first grade. His sister, Anne, nine, was in the fourth grade and Dow, the oldest, was a sixteen-year-old high school junior. It seemed like a good time to do what I'd wanted to do for years—go back to school. Actually doing so, even part-time, even as an auditor, was an awesome undertaking. I had graduated from college nineteen years earlier, and I wasn't sure I knew how to study or learn any more. If I looked as frightened as I felt those first weeks of class, people must have thought there was a five foot four inch scared rabbit running around campus!

With the encouragement of both professors and students, my fears dissolved. I discovered I could think and discuss intelligently. I realized that during years as an active church member and three years as a missionary, I had learned lessons, developed insights, and gathered experiences that were at least as valuable as the youth and the recent college diplomas most of the other students had. I welcomed the reading and written work for the course, and I welcomed the new ideas they stimulated in me.

After six or eight weeks of this encouragement, discovery, realization, and study, I suddenly thought, "Why am I auditing this course? I could graduate from seminary, just like those other students in my class. Why, I could even be ordained!"

Before telling anyone what I was thinking, I read the

115

requirements for seminary graduation. With the exception of Greek and Hebrew, they sounded like an excuse to do what I liked to do most—read, study, and work with people in the church. I figured I'd just have to endure Greek and Hebrew. Naïvely satisfied that I could get a Master of Divinity degree, the next thing I did was look in the Book of Church Order to see if a woman really could be a minister. In my forty years as a church member, I'd never seen one! And there it was, "in black and white." Ordination was open to people regardless of race, color, sex, age, or marital status.

The apparent simplicity of this changed when I began talking with seminary officials. They suggested I get a Master of Religion Arts degree, which the seminary was not yet offering, and prepare myself to work in Christian education. Or, perhaps, take the courses I wanted and become a more qualified lay leader. Or take some counseling courses, fulfill other requirements, and become a certified counselor. I was given little encouragement to get the standard degree given ministers. That strengthened my resolve to get that particular degree, even though at the time I did not see how I would use it.

Initially I met with less resistance to being ordained. Perhaps most people figured I'd never get far enough for that to be an issue! But the conviction was growing in me that I wanted to be a minister, and that God wanted me to be a minister—and that required ordination!

In one of the first courses I took after enrolling for the Master of Divinity degree, I did a lot of research about the role of women in the church. The more I learned about the history of women in the church, the more aware I became of the obstacles I would face if I were to become a minister.

Scheduling classes presented obstacles at first because I felt that I should take only courses that met while my children were in school. Also, I was strongly urged to go into Christian education, even though that was not my primary interest, because "a church might call a woman as minister of Christian education, but not as pastor." Field education placement was difficult. The pastor of the first church I interviewed decided his congregation just wasn't ready for a woman student. Fortunately, a member of presbytery's staff helped me get an invitation to preach a trial sermon for a small congregation needing a student for the summer. I had three wonderful months leading worship and preaching every Sunday, visiting, and surviving the trauma of my first funeral.

By graduation in 1974, I had gone over, around, and under other obstacles and survived other traumas. My family and I understood better what it would mean for me to be a full-time minister. I knew from experience the awkwardness of being a conspicuously visible minority at many church meetings. I flinched when it was assumed that ministers were all men. I had developed a firm biblical, theological, and experiential basis for my belief that I was called to be a minister.

A dilemma I had not resolved was whether I wanted to be a pastor of a church or a chaplain in an institution. I believed the call to ministry which would lead to my ordination would help resolve that dilemma. But the call was not being made. Ordination was nowhere in sight. In the Presbyterian Church one has to be called not only by God, but also by a congregation or some other agency presbytery recognizes. For months, God's call to me seemed to be a private conversation, something no one else heard or wanted to participate in.

And then, a miracle happened! An old, small, urban church in west Louisville asked me to preach a trial sermon. They had not had a full-time pastor for several years, and

117

they decided they wanted me in that role. I would have to have a housing allowance because the manse was too small, and they consented to that. My marriage was ending in divorce, but they agreed to call me as their pastor.

So being ordained Thanksgiving Sunday was most wonderfully appropriate. The congregation added their unique touch to the ordination service by giving me a bouquet of red roses. We celebrated communion together. When I served the bread and cup of the Eucharist, I was filled with thanksgiving for the encouragement of those who loved me, for the availability of a good seminary to study in, for my persistent conviction God wanted me to be a minister, for a congregation willing to call a woman, and for God's grace and guidance in bringing us together.

To be ordained during Pentecost was significant, also. It is a season of emphasis upon the presence of the Spirit, a season symbolized by green, the color of growth, and a season that promises dreams will be dreamed.

The congregation and I have grown together in the Spirit. Most of the members had voted to call me as their pastor, but there had been some who did not agree. Being faithful church members, they continued to participate and were willing to give me a chance. Their attitude was not so much that I had to prove myself, as it was that they would see how things worked out. I knew things were beginning to "work out" six months later, after my first Easter service, when I was told that one of the "loyal opposition" had said, "She's a fine preacher. We did the right thing in calling her." Another time, as I concluded a visit with a member in the hospital, she said, "Jane, there's something I need to say to you. I wasn't sure at first about having a woman minister, but I want you to know that now I *am* sure. I'm glad you are our pastor."

The fact that I am a woman minister is no longer a primary

118

issue for the congregation or for me. When the wife of a former minister of the church died, I went to visit the family and was introduced to several people I did not know. One of them said, "Oh, I've been wanting to meet you. I've never seen a woman minister before." An elder who had been on the session of Portland Avenue Presbyterian Church since I was ordained was standing nearby. He said, "Stand there for a minute and let me look at you. I never knew there was anything so unusual about a woman minister!" And I have become so accustomed to answering, "This is she," when people call the church and ask for the minister, that I have to remind myself that their silent response is probably surprise, because they are not accustomed to having a minister be "she."

One of my warmest affirmations as a pastor came when I visited an older member in the hospital. One of her sons was with her, and he asked me by what title I liked to be called. I said that "minister" and "Reverend" are used by a lot of folk, that pastor is my personal preference, and that what I like most to be called is "Jane." His mother immediately said, "Of course. You don't need anyone to tell you who you are. You know who you are."

In situations where change is needed, calling a woman minister is a distinct advantage. The decision itself represents such a change that the congregation may be willing to continue doing some things differently. The first few Sundays I was at Portland Avenue Presbyterian Church I did not wear a robe. I asked an elder how she thought the congregation would react to my wearing a light beige robe, rather than the traditional black. "After we voted to call a woman," she replied, "anything goes! Wear whatever color you want!"

The same strength and flexibility demonstrated when a

119

congregation calls a woman will help them follow her leadership in making other changes.

A friend who is a pastoral counselor asked me for a sociological description of the church and the neighborhood. After I gave it to him, he said, "It sounds like a matriarchy." I cringed, because a matriarchy is just as sexist and can be just as limiting as a patriarchy. I told him this, and he pointed out that probably many people I worked with were accustomed to women's using power indirectly and obliquely through other people, particularly through men who were in positions of authority. The opportunity I had as a woman pastor was to use power directly and openly from my position of authority. This helped me realize that this was what I was doing when I encouraged the session to involve the entire congregation in setting goals, when I got session approval of committee plans and my own plans, and when I presented my position on issues and invited—and received!—disagreement as well as agreement.

Something I had not expected as a minister was that I would be ministered to—be loved and cared for warmly by my family in faith. This has happened with birthday cards, wishes for a good vacation or a safe trip to a meeting, and concern when I have been sick. It happened beautifully when I married again and one of the women asked me if we wanted to have a reception. We wanted a very simple wedding, and we had decided that that included no reception. I explained this, and she nodded understandingly. In about five minutes, however, I was the one who understood—what she was really saying was that she would like to give us a reception! I went back to her, and she was enthusiastic about the reception and agreeable to my ideas of simplicity. When the wedding ceremony was over the reception began. It was lavish and loving and anything but simple! I was being ministered to!

Something a church may not expect when calling a woman pastor is that there will be attention and publicity for the congregation and for her. Most of this is favorable. An exception is anonymous crank letters quoting "proof texts" against the ordination of women. These are best thrown in the wastebasket.

More favorable are honest inquiries from friends of the congregation who ask, "How can a woman be a minister?" We have handled this question by inviting those friends and others to a series of Bible studies based on various difficult texts, including some of Paul's writings about women. Other good publicity has been occasional newspaper articles, television coverage of my ordination service, and continuing invitations for me to be on television and to talk with local groups.

Some doors are closed to a woman pastor, but being a woman pastor opens many other doors. Most boards, agencies, and committees of denominations are expected to have at least one or two women members. Some of this is tokenism. On the other hand, it helps our congregation to become involved in denominational matters through the pastor. That seldom happens to the small congregation served by a man. It also gives the woman minister an opportunity to serve with groups she probably would not have been invited to join for years, if she were a man. The boards, agencies, and committees gain the advantage of being more representative.

However, I had to learn early to say no when I knew I wasn't qualified or did not have the time, and to be selective about what I agreed to do. I also learned that it is easy to feel used and to lose, to become *the* advocate for equal employment opportunities, *the* spokesperson for what

121

women ministers think, *the* model of women in the ministry.

For that reason, it is a happy day when there are more than one or two women ministers in an area, and more than a few clergywomen who are members of a presbytery or similar church court. It is good for everyone to see that we come in all shapes and sizes, that we have different points of view, that we represent a variety of theological positions. My daughter was with me when I went to make a hospital visit. I remarked that the car we parked behind had a clergy sticker on it. "You mean 'clergyman,'" she corrected me. "Where do you get that clergy*man* business?" I asked. "How can you be sure that car belongs to a man?" "Because ninety-nine percent of clergy are men, and I've got the other one percent right here beside me!" she answered. It will be good when her percentages are no longer correct.

Dreams are part of Pentecost along with growth and the presence of the Spirit. I have dreamed many dreams since I first thought about being ordained. Some of the dreams have been nightmares. A few have been real-life nightmares! One was the day I reported to presbytery on a synod meeting and declared I hoped the time would come when synod no longer would be predominantly white, male, and middle-aged. After I sat down, I heard a white, middle-aged male say, "Boy, has she got problems!" Another was the time a close associate said he hoped a student couple would attend church and hear me preach because the woman needed a role model—no word about my worship leadership or preaching ability. A third was the time I overheard a search committee I was going to interview say (not knowing I was behind them in the hall), "Well, this next interview is a waste of time. Everyone knows we are not going to call a woman."

Some of my good dreams are that congregations and

search committees will become as much at ease with the fact that a candidate is a woman as the woman herself is, and will be able to give their full attention to her qualities as a prospective pastor who may be the best *person* their congregation could call. Another of my good dreams is that clergywomen, particularly those who are "solo" or single staff pastors, and their male peers in similar positions, will more easily develop collegial relationships with each other for support and encouragement. I also dream of the time when women will be called to small churches with potential for ministry and growth, as well as to small churches with little hope. I dream that women ministers who are not married, or not married to other pastors, will be as attractive to pulpit nominating committees as clergy couples whose attraction, unconsciously, may be that the husband of the couple "validates" the wife's ministry. And I dream of the time when a book about women in the ministry will be an anachronism!

Contributors

Maribeth Blackman-Sexton is a native of Oklahoma, and from January 1978 through August 1981 she served as the minister of the First Christian Church in the farming community of Walters, Oklahoma. In the summer of 1981, she accepted a call to serve as Associate Regional Minister of the Christian Church (Disciples of Christ) in Indiana.

Ellen Brubaker is a long-time friend and ministerial colleague of Marjorie Swank Matthews. Ellen serves as a minister in the West Michigan Conference of The United Methodist Church, and since June, 1971, has been the pastor of the Belding United Methodist Church.

Dorothy Nell Fowler was the first woman to be appointed as a part-time local pastor in the New Mexico Conference of The United Methodist Church. She teaches government at Permian High School in Odessa, Texas, and since 1976 has served as the pastor of the First United Methodist Church of Wink, Texas.

Mary Sue Gast received the D. Min. degree from Chicago Theological Seminary in 1975. She served with her husband, Roger D. Straw, as campus minister at Iowa State University from 1975 to 1978. They served as co-pastors of the First Congregational United Church of Christ in Union City, Michigan from 1978 to 1981—when they accepted a call to serve as pastors of the Smith Memorial United Church of Christ in Grand Rapids, and as coordinators of the Riverside Project, an educational ministry concerned with peace and disarmament.

Jane Krauss Jackson, the first woman ordained to be a full-time pastor by the Presbytery of Louisville (Union), completed a seven-year pastorate at Portland Avenue Presbyterian Church, Louisville, and in July 1981, she accepted a call to be the pastor of the Jeffersontown Presbyterian Church.

Carolyn J. Jones accepted a call in 1977 to become the associate pastor of the Glenshaw Presbyterian Church (UPCUSA) in suburban Pittsburgh, Pennsylvania. Previously she had taught English in the United States and overseas, and she also served as Assistant Dean of Women at Syracuse University, where she earned a Master's degree in personnel administration.

Barbara Jurgensen, the first woman in the Illinois District of the American Lutheran Church to be *the* pastor of a congregation in that District, has been serving as the pastor of First Lutheran Church of Logan Square in Chicago since August 1978. She is the wife of a Lutheran pastor, the mother of three, a prolific author, and a doctoral candidate in Old Testament at the Divinity School of the University of Chicago.

Mary Miller-Vikander served four years with Youth for Christ, International, and returned to school to earn the M. Div. degree at North Park Theological Seminary. In 1980, after serving as a pastor and hospital chaplain in her hometown of Rockford, Illinois, she was called to be the Associate Pastor of Faith Covenant Church in Farmington Hills, Michigan. She also serves as Vice-President of the

Ministerial Conference of the Great Lakes Conference of the Evangelical Church of America.

Anne Plunkett Rosser has been serving since September 1979, with her husband, Aubrey, as co-pastor of the Bainbridge-Southampton Baptist Church (SBC) in Richmond, Virginia. She was the first woman pastor in the Southern Baptist Convention to receive the D. Min. degree.

Lyle E. Schaller is the Parish Consultant on the staff of Yokefellow Institute, Richmond, Indiana. He is an ordained minister in The United Methodist Church, the author of twenty books, and the general editor of Abingdon's Creative Leadership Series.

Janet Gifford-Thorne was called in March of 1975 to become the pastor of the Plumbrook Baptist Church (ABC) in Sterling Heights, Michigan. A native of Oregon and a graduate of Colgate Rochester Divinity School, Janet has emphasized the empowerment of both the laity and the clergy in her ministry.

Ansley Coe Throckmorton is the Senior Minister of the Hammond Street Congregational Church (UCC), in Bangor, Maine, since 1978. In 1981, she was one of the recipients of the Antoinette Brown award of the United Church of Christ. She will also serve in 1982 as the President of the Maine Conference of the United Church of Christ.